·A·REVOLUTION·IN· ·LONDON·HOUSING·

LCC HOUSING ARCHITECTS & THEIR WORK
1893-1914

D1580711

·A·REVOLUTION·IN· ·LONDON·HOUSING·

LCC HOUSING ARCHITECTS & THEIR WORK
1893-1914

Susan Beattie

Greater London Council

The Architectural Press: London

First published in Great Britain by
The Greater London Council in
association with The Architectural Press Ltd.

© Department of Architecture and Civic Design,
Greater London Council 1980.

ISBN 0 85139 560 0

Produced in the Department of Architecture
and Civic Design, Greater London Council.

Architect to the Council
F B Pooley CBE

Surveyor of Historic Buildings
B Ashley Barker

Section Head, Survey and General
John Earl

Graphics and Book Design
John Beake

Editorial Control
David Atwell, Departmental Information Officer, to whom any
enquiries regarding the contents of this book should be addressed.

Printed and bound in Great Britain
for GLC Supplies Department
by Redwood Burn Ltd 34987 1/1980 (2000)

·CONTENTS·

·ACKNOWLEDGEMENTS·

The author wishes to thank the following for the help they gave during the research for this book: Gloria Clifton, A S Gray, Godfrey Rubens, Andrew Saint, Robert Thorne, Joyce Winmill.

Acknowledgements for photographs

The following have kindly given permission for the reproduction of photographs in their possession:

Plate 7   Robert Thorne

Plate 28   Sir John Bowman

Plates 29, 30, 39, 141, 152, 156, 161, 162 and 169   Royal Institute of British Architects

All other photographs are the copyright of the Greater London Council.

Abbreviations used in text and notes

AA   Architectural Association.

GLRO   Greater London Record Office.

LCC   London County Council.

RIBA   Royal Institute of British Architects.

RIBA Library, Recommendations . . .   Nomination papers for licentiate or associate membership of the Institute.

SPAB   Society for the Protection of Ancient Buildings.

Except where otherwise stated original working drawings mentioned in the text are retained at County Hall.

·FOREWORD·

The Greater London Council's Historic Buildings Committee has always accepted that the dissemination of historical informatton about London is one of its duties and members feel that at least some of the work done for them should be made available in published form. In recent years the Committee has encouraged the completion of a number of important pieces of research.

This book on the work of the first LCC housing architects was in fact completed by the author some time after she had left the Council's service and I am particularly grateful to Susan Beattie for her generosity in giving so much of her time to this project.

The history of the housing of the working classes by philanthropic companies and public authorities has engaged social historians for some time and a number of books on the subject have appeared in recent years. This monograph, however, is the first architectural account of an aspect of that movement. The common tendency to dismiss many of the earliest blocks of dwellings as grim pieces of prison architecture is not altogether without some justification. What the author demonstrates in this book is that in one office at the turn of the century, architectural and social values went hand in hand. The names of the young men involved, Reginald Minton Taylor, Owen Fleming, Charles Canning Winmill, Arthur Maxwell Philips and their colleagues are still virtually unknown (an inevitable consequence of having spent most of their working lives as public servants) but they were undoubtedly in the forefront of architectural progress and their buildings are ornaments to London. The quality of two of their most pleasing estates, Boundary and Millbank, has been recognized by the Secretary of State for the Environment, who has rightly included them in his statutory list of buildings of special architectural or historic interest.

The period covered by the book witnessed the important contribution made by these young architects to the Arts and Crafts movement in England inspired by William Morris. It was William Morris who founded the Society for the Protection of Ancient Buildings and it is not without significance that the London County Council almost from its inception took a keen interest in recording and preserving London's historic buildings. The work of the Council's housing architects was informed by both social and historical influences. The movement was sadly short-lived and ended with the outbreak of the first world war.

I am glad that one of the unexpected benefits to come from this research has been the revelation that nearly all the original design and detail drawings for these early estates have survived in the Plan Room at County Hall. They are outstanding examples of the architectural draughtsmanship of their time, boldly executed on stout cartridge paper with strong washes of colour and lively, stylised lettering. With the transfer of housing to the London boroughs this collection is now being partly dispersed but steps are being taken to ensure that the material will still be available to researchers. We owe it to Taylor, Fleming, Winmill and their fellow architects to see that we do not lose sight of these records and we recognise that we have a duty to future generations to see that their buildings are properly cared for.

I hope that Susan Beattie's book will help to release these men from eighty years of anonymity. She tells the story with skill and enthusiasm and shows how architects such as Webb and Lethaby influenced them in their work.

This volume, the latest in the growing number of publications by members of our staff, is to be welcomed. It will fill an important gap in our programme of research and I am sure that it will appeal to the general reader as well as all interested in architecture and its links with social history.

William Bell
Chairman, GLC Historic Buildings Committee

·1·

·INTRODUCTION·

In the spring of 1893 a new group was formed within the Architect's Department of the London County Council and called the Housing of the Working Classes Branch after the committee it served. It became, almost overnight, the dominant force within the Department, a breeding ground for architectural design of a peculiarly rational and elegant kind. Moreover, it has earned for the Council's building programme between 1893 and 1914 the right to be counted among the highest achievements of the Arts and Crafts movement in English architecture. That a group of young and exceptionally talented architects, recently trained, enthusiastic and like-minded, should have been at hand to fill the jobs in the new branch might seem at first impression to have been mere happy co-incidence. Yet these men were themselves a part of the tide of social consciousness upon which the issue of working class housing had first been raised. Excited by the socialist philosophy of William Morris and its archi-tectural expression in the buildings of Philip Webb and the teaching and writing of W R Lethaby, they under-stood how radically the stark and terrible predicament of the poor in Victorian cities could be changed by architec-tural means. Morris, Webb and Lethaby had provided the principles and the inspiration and had continued to design for the rich: the story of LCC housing before the first world war is the story of how the leap from theory to practice was made.

Housing was neither the only nor the first branch of the LCC Architect's Department to be called upon to produce designs for new buildings, though during the years immediately after the creation of the Council in 1889 most of the Architect's responsibilities were administrative and not constructional. The office of Architect and the struc-ture of his department had their origin in the Metropolitan Board of Works, the LCC's predecessor as London's governing authority. The first Superintending Architect of Metropolitan Buildings was Frederick Marrable who took up his appointment, shortly after the inaugural meeting of the Board in 1856, at a salary of £800 a year, with two clerks to assist him. He was to resign early in 1861 after a fruitless attempt to get his salary raised by more than £200. Marrable's duties, which he took pains to list in full in his letter of resignation to the Board, were related chiefly 'to the Survey, Valuation and Purchase of property for the New Streets undertaken by the Board'.[1] He was able to cite only one instance of having been called upon to design and superintend the erection of a building: the Board's new offices in Spring Gardens near Trafalgar Square, a dignified if conventional Italianate 'palace', inherited by the LCC, superseded by the present County Hall on the South Bank in 1919, and now demolished (Plate 1).

In March 1861 the architect George Vulliamy was appointed to replace Marrable at a salary of £1,000 a year. By 1865 he had accumulated a staff of twelve includ-ing a principal clerk, surveyor, draughtsmen and assistant clerks of various grades, but still had no important con-

structional work in his charge. The design of the great pumping stations, symbols of the Board's pioneering sewerage system, was the work of engineers and, curiously, the first long-term building programme of architectural significance that came within Metropolitan Board of Works control originated not in the Architect's Department, but the Fire Brigade. The Board took over responsibility for the London Fire Brigade Establishment from the Insurance Companies in 1866 and three years later a principal assistant clerk, Edward Cresy, was given the official title of Architect to the Fire Brigade, his salary to be split between his two functions: £500 as Clerk and £200 as Architect. Cresy died in 1870 and in 1871 his post was filled by Alfred Mott, first recruited to the Engineer's Department as a draughtsman in 1858. From 1871 Mott is described in the Board's staff lists as 'Assistant Surveyor, Architect's Department'. He was no revolutionary designer as the early fire stations built under his superintendence show (Plate 2), but in March 1879 a new draughtsman named Robert Pearsall was appointed to his staff. Though his name is scarcely known today, Pearsall deserves better for it was he who transformed the plain brick shell of the '70s into a Gothic fantasy rich with spires and turrets and robustly detailed decorative stonework (Plates 3-4).

In February 1887, on the retirement of Vulliamy, the Board made its third and final choice of Superintending

Architect, a choice that was to have far-reaching consequences for the LCC. Thomas Blashill, like W E Riley after him, had a remarkable gift for recognising design abilities in others while his own remained well concealed behind his official duties. Owen Fleming, one of his chief assistants was to declare in 1900, 'of the Council's late Superintending Architect, Mr Blashill, it is impossible to speak without enthusiasm. The confidence he placed in us younger men, often in the face of a good deal of public criticism, has endeared him to us in perhaps a special degree, and it has been an honour for us to have been

---

1 (*above*)
Old County Hall, Spring Gardens, Westminster. Designed by Frederick Marrable, 1860. (Demolished.)
2 (*facing page, top left*)
Old Greenwich Fire Brigade Station. Designed by Alfred Mott, 1879. (Demolished.) From an LCC photograph.
3 (*facing page, top right*)
Former Fire Brigade Station, Bishopsgate, City. Designed by Robert Pearsall, 1884. From the print in the Architect's Plan Room, County Hall.
4 (*facing page, bottom*)
Fire Brigade Station, 685. Fulham Road, Hammersmith. Designed by Robert Pearsall, 1896.

selected to assist him in the execution of the greatest work [the Council's housing programme] of his public career'.[2] Blashill was born in Yorkshire in 1831 and became a pupil of T E Knightley, the architect in the 1890s of Birbeck's Penny Bank in Holborn. He took an active part on the committees and Council of the RIBA and was elected President of the Architectural Association in 1862. Until 1887 he was working as a district surveyor. 'He had also abilities as a draughtsman and in water-colour work which few who knew him only as a high public official ever suspected', wrote one of his colleagues at the time of his death in 1905.[3]

When Blashill took over the Board's Architect's Department it was staffed by some seventy people divided between seven branches: the Building Act branch, Improvements, Compensation and Estates branch (later Works and Improvements), Parks and Open Spaces, Fire Brigade, Dangerous Structures, Street Nomenclature and Theatres. Of these, Fire Brigade was the only one concerned primarily with the design and construction of new buildings. The transfer of the powers of the Metropolitan Board of Works to the London County Council following the Local Government Act of 1888 took place in March 1889, causing little or no reverberation in Blashill's Department. The only important staff changes that he made immediately were, in 1890, the promotion of Robert Pearsall to principal in the Fire Brigade branch and the recruitment of a student and fellow member of the AA, Owen Fleming, onto the temporary staff of the Works and Improvement branch at three guineas a week. However, a more momentous event took place at this time that, as Blashill must have realised, would profoundly affect the character of his Department. Amid a rising clamour of protest against the appalling living conditions of the poor in cities, the Housing of the Working Classes Act was passed in 1890 and the Public Health and Housing Committee of the LCC set up to carry out London's responsibilities under the Act.

From 1851, the year of Lord Shaftesbury's 'Common Lodging House Act', attempt after legislative attempt had been made to deal with the colossal problem of slum housing, though responsibility for actually building homes for the poor at cheap rents had rested firmly with private enterprise and philanthropic bodies, notably the Peabody Trust, the Improved Industrial Dwellings Company and the East End Dwellings Company. The Metropolitan Board of Works had no powers to erect new housing, only to buy up and clear slum areas and then to sell them by auction, on condition that homes for the poor would be provided on the same or nearby sites. Critics were not slow to point out that this system lent itself to misapplication and even deliberate abuse. Joseph Chamberlain protested, in the *Fortnightly Review*, that all Acts of Parliament concerned with housing were virtually a directive to bad landlords 'to allow your property to fall into disrepair, to become a nest of diseases, and a centre of crime and immorality, and then we will step in and buy it from

you at a price seventy per cent above what you could obtain in the ordinary market if you attempted to dispose of it without our assistance'.[4] Once in possession of a cleared site the Board was naturally in no position to demand a high price for it and was even expected to provide indirect subsidy for housing by selling it cheaply. In the face of the dwellings companies' rapidly rising costs of labour and building materials the possibility of selling it at all was steadily diminishing. And how, in the event of a rebuilding programme actually beginning, was the problem of overcrowding to be properly tackled when the legislation required the Board to rehouse all the people displaced by slum clearance *on the same site*? A striking example of the malfunction of such a system is the Great Wild Street scheme. A slum area with a population of 1,839 and a death rate of about forty in a thousand, bounded by Drury Lane, Kemble Street and the now renamed Wild Street, Westminster, was bought by the Board in 1879 for £121,266 and cleared of buildings. The Board sold to the Peabody Trustees the following year for £15,840, with the proviso that 1,939 people be rehoused upon the site, 240 of whom should be accommodated in one lodging house. To make matters worse, and the proposed density even higher, the site area was to be reduced to allow for street widening. The Trustees, unable to meet the impossible rehousing requirement, compromised by providing homes for 1,620 people and that only by building to the exceptional height of six storeys. 'It will be seen', ran the official account of the development, 'that . . . the area was not sufficiently extensive for the purpose'. The estate which still stands today was designed by the Trustees' architect, Henry Darbishire, and may fairly be taken to represent the architectural norm for working class housing before the LCC architects entered the field in 1893 (Plate 5). Though, as J N Tarn has argued, 'when such a redevelopment as this is criticised today, the pressure which was brought to bear on the architect should not be forgotten',[5] the attitude to poverty implicit in this and other such dwellings, rigidly uniform, forbidding and 'closed' in aspect (see, for example, Plate 6), was nevertheless to be vigorously rejected by Blashill's staff working under similarly difficult conditions. It was rejected too by all who were concerned with improving the plight of the poor and who, interestingly enough, had no hesitation at all in identifying the miseries of working class people with their architectural environment. The feelings of horror and disgust that the subject evoked are eloquently expressed by George Gissing in his description of a flatted estate built by the

---

5 (*facing page, top*)
Peabody Estate, Kemble Street, Westminster. Designed by Henry Darbishire, 1881.
6 (*facing page, bottom*)
Guinness Trust Estate, Columbia Road, Tower Hamlets. Designed by F T Pilkington, 1892.

Metropolitan Association for Improving the Dwellings of the Industrious Classes (Plate 7): 'What terrible barracks, those Farringdon Road buildings: Vast, sheer walls, unbroken by even an attempt at ornament; row above row of windows in the mud-coloured surface, upwards, upwards, lifeless eyes, murky openings that tell of bareness, disorder, comfortlessness within. . . . An inner courtyard, asphalted, swept clean – looking up to the sky as from a prison. Acres of these edifices, the tinge of grime declaring the relative dates of their erection; millions of tons of brute brick and mortar, crushing the spirit as you gaze. Barracks, in truth; housing for the army of industrialism, an army fighting with itself, rank against rank, man against man, that the survivors may have whereon to feed. Pass by in the night, and strain imagination to picture the weltering mass of human weariness, of bestiality, of un-merited dolour, of hopeless hope, of crushed surrender, tumbled together within those forbidding walls.'[6]

Nor does the starry-eyed idealism of Octavia Hill's views on the block dwelling and its influence on human character obscure their powerful appeal. 'The first senti-mental objection to the block life', she wrote in 1889, 'is the small scope it gives for individual freedom. The second is its painful ugliness and uninterestingness in external look which is nearly connected with the first. For difference is at least interesting and amusing, monotony never. Let us hope that when we have secured our drainage, our cubic space of air, our water on every floor, we may have time to live in our homes, to think how to make them pretty, each in our own way, and to let the individual characteristics they take from our life in them be all good as well as healthy and beautiful, because all human work and life were surely meant to be like all Divine creations, lovely as well as good'.[7]

By the 1890s the type of Farringdon Buildings and the Peabody Estate at Drury Lane was so widespread that any housing scheme of five storeys or more, of whatever quality, was instantly pronounced 'barrack-like' and unsuitable for civilised life. Ernest Dewsnup observed in 1907, 'Block dwellings are common enough in some countries but have never appealed to English taste, not-withstanding that at least from four to five thousand of such dwellings are in existence in London and the pro-vinces.'[8] Against such a background – of anger and reform-ing fervour, political manoeuvring and simple prejudice – the new London County Council took over London's housing problem from the Board in 1889, together with a number of sites already cleared for housing purposes that were proving impossible to sell. It was obvious that the Board's housing policy was at a standstill. Determined to act more positively the LCC urged the Government to consolidate all previous legislation relating to working class housing and to make firm provision for it to be built if necessary by local authorities themselves.

Equipped with the new powers accorded by the Housing of the Working Classes Act of 1890 and faced with its own repeated failures to sell two plots of land inherited

from the Board at Brook Street, Limehouse, the Council resolved, on 5 April 1892, 'itself to erect dwellings on the sites and obtained the consent of the Secretary of State to this course'.[9] The first outcome of this historic decision was the erection of Beachcroft Buildings, a small develop-ment of four-storey tenement blocks off Cable Street, Limehouse (Plate 8). Their design pre-dates the formation of the Housing branch of the Architect's Department. Authority was given to the Architect to employ a tem-porary assistant to handle the Brook Street scheme in December 1892 and the drawings would have been made in the Works and Improvements branch where the first young men recruited to carry out the functions of the Public Health and Housing Committee congregated in the course of 1892 and the early weeks of 1893. Though at first glance today Beechcroft Buildings may not seem to depart very far from the grim utilitarianism of private enterprise working class housing, nevertheless in certain respects they clearly reflect the LCC's determination to alleviate the most harsh characteristics of the type. Project-ing bays are introduced to break up the stark pattern of flatly repeating window units, and, if only by varying the pattern of light and shade across the façade, to suggest that some degree of difference and individuality might exist among the identically-planned tenements. Most important of all, though soon to be reversed, was the policy of reducing the building height. Inspired by the common dread of 'barrack' dwellings, there was a Government move, about 1890, to restrict the height of blocks to four storeys, a move strongly supported by the LCC. But the so-called '3 per cent resolution' of March 1893 was to make such improvements economically impossible: 'The rents to be charged for the dwellings erected in connection with any specified housing scheme or area shall not exceed those ruling in the neighbourhood, and shall be so fixed that after providing for all outgoings, interest and sinking fund charges, *there shall be no charge on the county rate* [author's italics] in respect of the dwellings on such area or scheme, and all such dwellings shall be so designed that the cost of erection may not exceed a sum which will enable the Council to carry out the foregoing conditions. The interest and sinking fund charges shall be calculated upon the cost of erection, plus the value of the site, subject to the obligation to build dwellings for the working classes upon it'.[10] In 1896 the Architect, reporting on the feasibility of building even to a height of six storeys, recalled the

---

7 (*facing page, top left*)
Farringdon Buildings, Farringdon Road, Islington. Designed by Frederick Chancellor, 1874. (Demolished.)
8 (*facing page, bottom*)
Beachcroft Buildings, Cable Street, Tower Hamlets. 1892-3. (Demolished.)
9 (*facing page, top right*)
Yabsley Street flats, Poplar, Tower Hamlets. 1894. (Demolished.)

Council's early attempts to conform to the same restrictions as it had attempted to impose on others. 'The first building erected, viz Beechcroft Buildings, Limehouse, was four storeys only in height. It was, however, a very expensive building. The working drawings for Yabsley Street were also prepared on the same basis, but it was found that the cost of four-storey Dwellings was incompatible with the provision of the sanitary and other requirements that the Council desired in their Buildings. Consequently the Public Health and Housing Committee, on 16 January 1893, recommended to the Council that five storeys should be substituted for four . . . '.[11] It is interesting to see how the Housing branch dealt with the additional storey when, reluctantly, it was adopted at the Yabsley Street flats in Poplar (Plate 9). The introduction of an attic treated with originality as a conspicuous element in the design stresses the sculptural quality of the blocks and, far from emphasising, actually helps to reduce the impression of overwhelming bulk that public opinion had turned so vigorously against.

By 1893 the pressure on Thomas Blashill's Department to produce designs and supervise building works for the Public Health and Housing Committee was too great to be borne any longer by a few specially recruited young assistants in the Works and Improvements branch. 'It has been found very inconvenient to confine these assistants to the particular buildings or works on which they are engaged', reported the Architect through the appropriate committee. 'They should', he recommended, 'be grouped together so that each may undertake that particular class of work for which he is, in the opinion of the Architect, best suited'.[12] In March 1893 the Establishment Committee reported on the need to appoint onto the permanent staff 'certain officers hitherto temporarily employed in connection with housing schemes', and concluded, 'in view of the fact that this work seems to have become an established portion of his [the Architect's] duties . . . it would be well that a separate branch of his department should be formed, and that certain temporary men be allotted permanently to this branch'.[13]

·2·

·THE·ARCHITECTS· ·OF·BOUNDARY· ·STREET·AND· ·MILLBANK·

The first men appointed to staff the new Housing of the Working Classes Branch were Owen Fleming, T G Charlton, R Robertson, R M Taylor, W Hynam and H R Ward. The arrival of C C Winmill and A M Philips shortly afterwards completed the group that, with the exception of Ward who died in 1896 and Charlton who left in the same year, formed the nucleus of the branch until the re-organisation of the Department under Blashill's successor in 1900–1. All except Taylor and Ward had been students in the design classes at the Architectural Association which was then fast gaining ground on the Royal Academy as London's foremost school of architecture.

It seems probable that the identification of separate hands in the work produced by the branch is a problem that will never be satisfactorily solved. The prospect of discovering some branch file that had both miraculously escaped destruction and broken the inflexible policy of anonymity is extremely remote. My own attempts to unravel the threads of individual style in Council architecture have been governed principally by the initials of examining architects that appear on most of the surviving contract drawings: it seems reasonable to assume that an architect who oversaw the making of a group of drawings held at least some responsibility for design on that project. Indeed, independent evidence has occasionally been found to support this assumption. Yet the buildings themselves are the greatest impediments of all to the recognition of their separate designers for they are the living expression of the corporate identity of the Housing branch. United by their idealism, committed to Morris's vision of social reform and to the abolition of the double standard, compelled for economic reasons to look long and hard at the relationship between form and function in building and to abandon elaborate tricks of style, the designers of LCC working class housing brought English architecture as close as it ever came to the radicalism of W R Lethaby.

The formation of the Housing branch coincided with a period of change and excitement in London's architectural circles. That burning debate, 'Architecture: a Profession or an Art', to which Lethaby had contributed, reached its climax in the publication of the book of the same title in 1892 and in the 1890s William Morris's Society for the Protection of Ancient Buildings was at the height of its effectiveness, not only in conservation but as a breeding ground for the theories and aspirations of an architectural élite. Its membership in the '90s reads like a roll call of the most eminent Arts and Crafts designers. Philip Webb, Lethaby, Thackeray Turner, William Morris, Emery Walker, George Jack, Ernest Gimson and J J Stevenson were among those on the committee in 1893. Ordinary members included the designer Walter Crane, the sculptors George Frampton and Hamo Thornycroft, Ernest Newton and Arthur Lasenby Liberty. 'It is a curious fact', wrote Lethaby later, 'that this Society, engaged in an intense study of antiquity, became a school of rational builders and modern building'.[14] The appearance of Charles Canning Winmill on the committee in 1898 was to

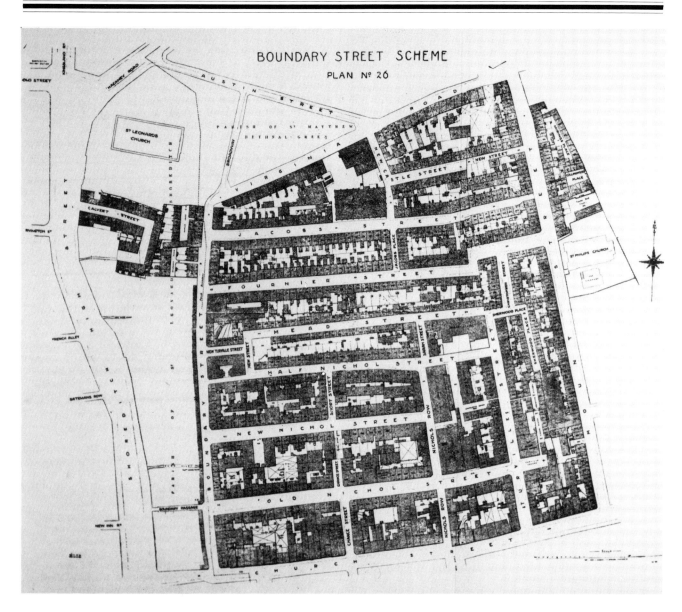

establish a direct link with the LCC, but the Housing branch staff had long been peculiarly open to the Society's influence. In 1894 Lethaby was appointed Art Inspector to the Technical Education Board of the LCC which was at that time considering the possibility of setting up a school of architecture (an idea that did not materialise but led to the foundation of the Central School of Arts and Crafts in 1896 with Lethaby and George Frampton as Principals). The following year he delivered two lectures at Bolt Court, specially addressed to architects and their pupils, on the subject of 'Modern Building Design in connexion with the work of the Technical Education Board of the LCC'. The lectures advocated a new asceticism in architecture. Classical ornaments and features should be laid aside and building construction reduced to its simplest form and developed anew.[15] Arthur Bolton of the Architectural Association, which saw the proposed new school as something of a threat to its own recently-won territory, was provoked to sarcastic comment: 'The improvement . . . of society is, doubtless, included in the

Curriculum of the Positive School of Architecture, and when the new heaven and earth of the LCC comes to pass, the new architecture will be there to house it'.[16]

The first decisive step in the direction of the LCC's 'new heaven', testing ground for the housing architects' social and architectural principles and inspiration of countless later housing schemes, was the Boundary Street Estate at Bethnal Green. The site was the Old Nichol, the terrible slum area immortalised in Arthur Morrison's book of 1896, *A Child of the Jago*, where the infant mortality rate was one in four, and where 'in subterranean basements men and women have swarmed and bred and died like wolves in their lairs', at each hopeless attempt at piecemeal improvement emerging from the foul old houses 'in clouds of choking dust, each . . . a colony of vermin'. (Plate 10). A comprehensive scheme for the clearance and redevelopment of the Old Nichol was approved by the Council as early as November 1890.[17] The news was received joylessly by an architectural press quick to react against the idea of a new rash of block dwellings. 'Of course,' reasoned

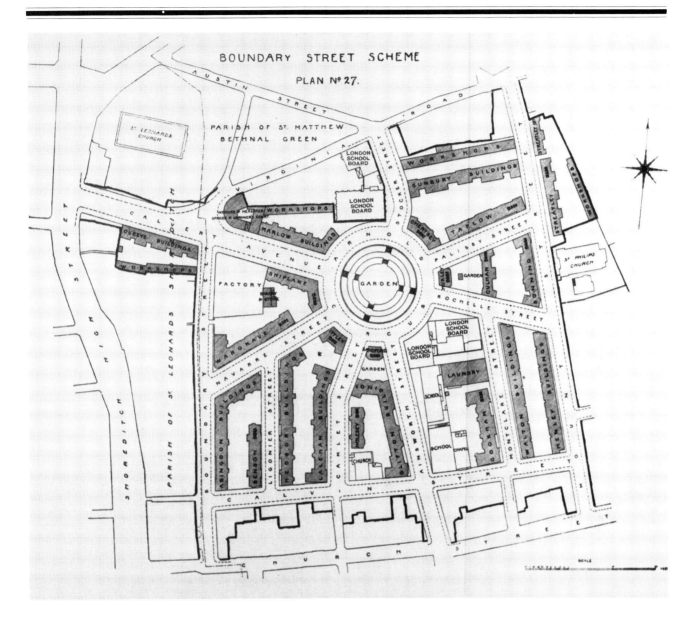

The Builder, 'the glamour about the County Council's scheme is that it promises a great work of improvement to be carried out comparatively promptly: and no wonder this attracts people who are wearied with the slow progress of sanitary reform in London. Perhaps it may be as well that this large experiment should be tried but the drawbacks to it already suggested must not be forgotten, besides another which very few people are alive to: viz: that not only has the building of lofty blocks of barrack-like dwellings a very depressing effect on the appearance of a neighbourhood, but that the crowding of the same number of people in tall blocks of buildings with a certain minimum space between them may be nearly as unhealthy as crowding them in lower houses more closely set. Over-crowding vertically is very little better than overcrowding laterally: it is only another way of arranging the same number of people on an area too small for them'.[18] The British Architect was apprehensive too, warning that 'we are all getting very weary of those severely plain, not to say dreary-looking structures which remind one rather of

Pentonville than the cosy home of the well-to-do artisan'.[19]

The original scheme had been to lay out new streets forty feet wide, on a rectangular grid pattern, providing for blocks arranged in the all-too-familiar parallel rows. But during the interval taken up with the purchase of land and demolition of the old houses a new idea emerged: to give the estate a centralised plan, the blocks arranged along tree-lined avenues radiating from a central circus (Plate 11). It was found, moreover, that this modification 'would enable more and pleasanter accommodation to be provided

---

10 *(facing page)*
The 'Old Nichol' area of Bethnal Green before redevelopment by the LCC. From The Housing Question in London, *LCC, 1900, p 192.*
11 *(above)*
Block plan of the Boundary Street Estate, Tower Hamlets.
From The Housing Question in London, *LCC, 1900, p 196.*

at a slightly smaller cost'.[20] The principal approach road from Shoreditch High Street was to be sixty feet wide, the other six avenues each fifty feet wide and to economise on carting costs it was planned to use the earth displaced from the foundations to build a raised garden on the central plot. Three other public garden plots were to be provided between the blocks. Though there had to be an economic justification for every aspect of the new plan, the real significance of the changes lay firmly elsewhere. The architect in charge, Owen Fleming, described long afterwards how he and his assistants had fought for the central raised garden with its bandstand that would be visible from most of the five-storey blocks (Plate 12); had seen it as a unifying element in what was essentially a living community with character of its own, not merely a collection of dwellings in regimented yet meaningless proximity to each other. Around the central bandstand, he had imagined, courting couples from the estate would stroll on fine summer evenings while the band played[21] – a Utopian vision that colourfully summarises a fast-changing attitude to the poor and their proper environment and establishes too how eagerly the Housing architects adapted to their pioneering role when they discovered that no satisfactory precedents existed. 'One might have hoped', commented Blashill, 'that on any subject connected with

block dwellings valuable lessons could be learned from Continental cities, where large buildings, consisting of many tenements, are the rule. But after searching the chief of these cities, particularly in Germany, and consulting many books, I am surprised at the poor results. The favourite plan just now seems to be to put blocks or rows of workmen's flats in yards behind flats of a superior class, an arrangement opposed to all our ideals'.[22] The LCC in the 1890s provided a sympathetic setting for the growth of advanced ideas. Nearly two-thirds of the members of the first Council were 'progressives', among them Sidney Webb (elected Member for Deptford in 1892), John Burns and B F C Costelloe, whose particular concern was for the housing problem. As far as the Housing of the Working Classes branch was concerned, the political orientation of the group seems to have been set, appropriately, by Owen Fleming himself, head of the branch till 1900.

Fleming was born in 1867 and was articled to his architect father on the Isle of Wight in 1882. In 1886 he was employed for a short time as an improver in the office of Charles Beazley and Herbert W Burrows, and later worked

12   (above)
Bandstand, central garden, Boundary Estate.

as an assistant to George Bevan and Henry Dobb. Prizeman at the Architectural Association and South Kensington schools, he was on the committee of the AA from 1889 to 1891 and co-editor of *AA Notes*. During the same period he was London editor of *The American Architect*, probably the most influential foreign architectural journal of that day. On nomination as an Associate of the RIBA in 1891, following his appointment onto the staff of the Works and Improvements branch, he cited among his private works to date 'cottages and houses, Isle of Wight, Staines, Honor Oak, etc.,' the restoration of a pre-reformation vicarage at Alfriston and shops at Cranleigh.[23] One of Fleming's AA competition designs for a country hotel, illustrated in *AA Notes*[24], shows him to have been an unadventurous designer yet he was a perceptive critic, sensitive to change and sympathetic to new developments in architecture. 'We are passing away from the age of revivals', he wrote on the winning entry in the competition for Kelvingrove Art Galleries and Museum, Glasgow, 'and I would fain regard this design as a successful attempt to obtain a striking result by careful attention to the artistic grouping of the masses.... Much of its ultimate beauty will depend upon a careful choice of colour in the material and on the character of its detail'.[25] He might have been describing the designs about to be produced by his assistants for the Boundary Street Estate; certainly Lethaby would have understood such comments. The spirit of social reform in which Owen Fleming undertook his responsibilities as head of the Housing branch is reflected in an appreciation he wrote of his friend Lionel Curtis, private secretary to the Chairman of the Council. He admiringly stressed Curtis's 'patience and tenderness, his indifference to fatigue when public interests were involved, and his almost passionate reverence for all that makes life good in the highest sense of the term', and it is easy to imagine Fleming himself as a man of similar qualities. The two friends had met for the first time in the East End of London, Fleming recalled. 'He and I were on the same quest. We were oppressed by the chain of circumstances that had compelled so many of the poor to live in insanitary dwellings. We were trying to get to the bottom of things, and had each of us felt that settlement life hardly afforded those opportunities for intimate contact with the question that we were seeking. The present Bishop of London was the kindly instrument who brought us together, and we lived for some years in a flat in a block of model dwellings at Stepney . . . .'.[26] The experience made a deep impression upon the young architect and he began the LCC's housing programme with an acute and caring knowledge of the serious objections that could be raised to model dwellings of any kind. It was impossible, he told the AA in 1900, 'to contemplate with any sense of satisfaction the obligatory crowding together of whole families in two small rooms. The moral standard of life must in such cases be very low, and it would be futile to expect the reasonable physical development of children nurtured under such conditions. Moreover, the more serious events of life, such as illness, child-

birth and death, take place ordinarily in these rooms, for it must be remembered that the hospital accommodation of East London is far from commensurate with the needs of the population. As for intellectual development, what possibility is there for the creation of a reasonable interest in life?'.[27] Yet he carried his involvement beyond idealism. He prepared a paper on 'London Workmen, Their Education and Workmanship' (read at the AA in January 1894) and when speaking in 1900 at the RIBA on the rebuilding of Boundary Street, his testimony to 'the great body of skilled artificers who have striven to make this estate a model of good workmanship', is pure Lethaby in feeling. 'Personally', he declared, 'I feel a special sense of comradeship with the men who have actually worked on these buildings. Their continuous struggle forwards, despite those soul-destroying delays when materials urgently needed did not arrive, or arrived wrongly contrived; their perseverance, in the face of repeated storms and frosts, calls forth the most cordial recognition. If any members of this Institute are ever tempted to visit Boundary Street, and find the workmanship worthy of admiration, will they think of the silent unnamed workers, by whose patient labour this great structure has been built up?'[28]

'This great structure' was developed in five sections, involving the displacement of 5,719 people, and providing, it was intended, for the rehousing of 4,600, the difference to be absorbed by a small housing scheme in nearby Goldsmith's Row (see page 85) and by existing vacant accommodation in the surrounding suburbs. But the inspired gesture of the radial plan was not followed up immediately by a similarly inspired series of designs for individual dwellings. The Housing architects had not yet found their identity as a design group and Council policy itself was still ambivalent in the face of fickle public opinion. Two blocks of flats, one of four and one of five storeys, were designed in 1893 and built during 1894 by the Council's Works Department on Section A, a piece of land detached from the rest of the estate on the east side of Mount Street (now renamed Swanfield Street). Called Streatley Buildings – the Housing Committee having agreed to name all the blocks on the Estate after towns along the Thames – they were of spartan external appearance yet were fiercely criticised for their high cost (Plate 13). The Council was clinging to the hope of improving on the standards set by the majority of housing trusts, yet at the same time was pledged to carry the housing programme through without causing an increase in the rates. Each inch of space in dwellings, including communal corridors and stairways, had to be justifiable in terms of the rents that could reasonably be charged. Yet high rents would and frequently did exclude the very class of society for which the new tenements had been raised. The expense of Streatley Buildings had been incurred by an over-lavish use of space: only two flats had been provided on each floor and both of these were of the type, known as 'self-contained', where all the accommodation was behind the occupant's own front door. The cheaper and obviously

less desirable plan type established for working class dwellings was called 'associated' and provided for the sharing of sculleries or lavatories or both with other flats on the same landing.

The Housing branch was inevitably caught up in the intolerable dilemma that afflicted the Council's housing policy. On the one hand there was the precariously balanced and politically sensitive budget which had to be seen to govern Blashill's every activity. 'All we can do as architects', he said, 'is to exercise the most rigid economy in planning, in fittings and in finishings, with a good deal of reserve in the design of elevations. Besides this, ordinary materials and articles must be used in ordinary ways. An opportunity of designing a working man's dwelling is not the occasion for experiments which might be tried, in his absence, in the house of a colonial millionaire'.[29] Reporting in November 1893 on the class of building to be prepared for Section B, Blashill advised the Housing Committee: 'I am strongly of the opinion that the Committee will have to consider the abandonment of these self-contained tenements [in Streatley Buildings] which are beyond the ordinary scale of accommodation provided by Artizans' Dwellings Companies and I should be glad of instructions to design tenements which are more in accordance with the practice of such companies and, so far as I know, are perfectly sanitary and well constructed and complete as to the fittings in the rooms'.[30]

On the other hand presided the reforming spirit of the Council's progressive members, impatient to see their reforms put into operation. Owen Fleming, who held views that coincided with theirs and was less fettered than Blashill by the demands of office, took the opportunity to express his more idealistic approach during a discussion of the Architect's paper on block dwellings read at the AA in 1900. He 'rather differed from Mr Blashill as to the architectural appearance of such buildings', convinced, he said, that in the East End 'some attention should be given to (their) external appearance . . .; and that if this were done the inhabitants would appreciate it. Let his audience take a walk from Hackney to Bethnal Green, Mile End, Poplar or Bow, and they would see just a long row of dreary monotony, all the houses being precisely the same, without any sort of architectural feeling at all'. He thought 'the East-Ender desired something a little better than that'. He explained how the planning of LCC flatted housing estates had been 'a compromise all through', the associated tenement an economically expedient denial of the universal truth that it was 'very much more agreeable to a man to have the whole of his house within his own front door'.[31]

13 (*top*)
Streatley Buildings, Boundary Street Estate, 1893.
(Demolished.) From an LCC photograph.
14 (*bottom*)
Walton House, Boundary Street Estate. Designed by Rowland Plumbe, 1894.

The completion of Streatley Buildings left the Housing branch painfully aware that in neither an economic nor an architectural sense could these first blocks be considered a success. The little comment they provoked from the profession was to be cruelly scathing.[32] Fleming who, characteristically, was moved more by the architectural failure than by the over-spending, was inclined to blame the structure of the Architect's Department. 'If there is one lesson that can be drawn from this occurrence it is that architectural design is not possible when architects are being worked at high pressure night after night and when they are separated from one another in isolated rooms, too distant for adequate co-operation'.[33] It must have been with some grim satisfaction that the branch watched the failure – for startlingly similar reasons – of Henley and Walton Buildings on the south east corner of the estate (Plate 14). The Council felt that faster progress might be made if some of the dwellings at Boundary Street were to be designed by outside architects. A limited competition of six architects experienced in the field of artisans' housing was held in 1894. 'Unfortunately, however, the experiment did not realise all that had been expected of it. Indeed, the experience that the Council's architects went through in their first buildings was repeated by Mr Rowland Plumbe, the successful competitor, in a somewhat remarkable way. In each case the amount of money available was considered greater than it actually was. In each case it was determined to try the experiment of constructing only two self-contained tenements per landing. In each case the result was a substantial deficit instead of the surplus that might reasonably have been looked for. In each case the plainness of the external treatment failed to arouse public enthusiasm. . . .'[34] The competition experiment was not repeated at Boundary Street.

Towards the end of 1894 a laundry was designed to serve the estate and during the course of 1895 working drawings were produced for eight tenement blocks: Cleeve, Sonning, Culham, Marlow, Shiplake, Hurley, Sandford and Taplow Buildings. All except Taplow were refused by the Council's Works Department and put out to competitive tender. Working drawings for Sunbury and Chertsey Buildings (built by the Works Department) were executed early in 1896, for Iffley Buildings (put out to tender) in November of that year, and for Clifton, Molesey, Wargrave and Cookham Buildings in 1897. Drawings for Hedsor, Laleham, Benson and Abingdon Buildings date from the summer of 1898. The finishing of these four blocks at the end of the following year marked the completion of the estate.

The nineteen blocks designed by Housing branch that surround the Circus and line the radial streets are remarkable for the invention and variety of their architecture, for a fastidious attention to detail that embraces not only their principal façades but rear and side elevations too, as if in deliberate defiance of the rule of uniformity that had been imposed upon the poor by the charitable trusts. The most obviously picturesque group seems to have been chiefly

the work of Reginald Minton Taylor and, being also the most prominently situated, represents for most people the essential character of Boundary Street. It consists of Cleeve, Marlow and Shiplake Buildings fronting onto Calvert Avenue, the main approach road from Shoreditch High Street, and Chertsey, Hurley and Sandford Buildings that, with Iffley Buildings designed under the superintendence of another architect, form the building line round Arnold Circus itself (Plates 15–22). Any danger that such tall blocks clustered about the central area might have appeared dark and oppressive has been dispelled in a bold and effective manner. Taking the gables – actual expressions of the controversial but enforced fifth storey – as the keynote of the group, the architect has introduced within their crisp broad outlines a rhythmic pattern of stripes and rectangles that spread outwards and downwards, carrying colour and movement across each façade. The elements of the style adopted here for the first time by the Housing branch were not new: red and yellow bricks and terracotta dressings and bands, long segmental headed windows with white painted sashes and frames almost flush with the wall surface, flat pilasters and gables and complex roof lines with cunningly articulated tall chimneys had all, by 1895, become commonplaces in a city that sparkled with the red brick and terra-cotta houses of the so-called Queen Anne Revival and the Board schools of E R Robson (Plates 23–24). The 'Queen Anne' house, however, as designed by Norman Shaw and his followers, and such blocks of flats as his Albert Hall Mansions or W H Powell's apartments in Mayfair (Plate 25) that bear some stylistic comparison with Boundary Street, were unequivocally for the rich and it is an interesting reflection on the paternalistic attitudes of the Victorians that the poor should have first been allowed to enjoy this essentially domestic architectural style not in their homes but at school. Nevertheless Robson himself had recognised the much wider significance of the 'Board School style' and its relevance to the problem of working class housing. In two essays on 'Art as Applied to Town Schools' he had outlined in 1881 an approach to architecture which reads like a manifesto of the LCC Housing branch and is echoed throughout their early building programme.[35]

'Architectural art', he wrote, depends intimately upon good workmanship, and upon applying rightly each material according to its nature. Common building needs first of all, to be closely looked to. Hordes of workmen,

15 (overleaf, left)
Shiplake House, from the central garden.
16 (overleaf, top right)
Shiplake House. Plans, showing the self-contained type. From the original working drawing dated July 1895.
17 (overleaf, bottom right)
Shiplake House. Elevations. From the original working drawing dated July 1895.

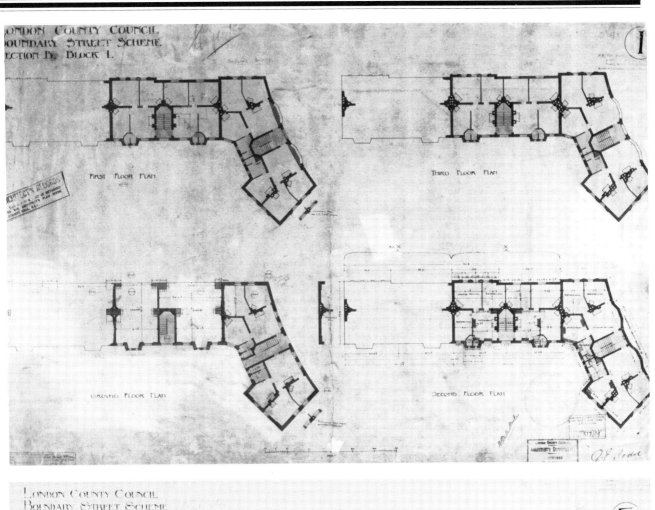

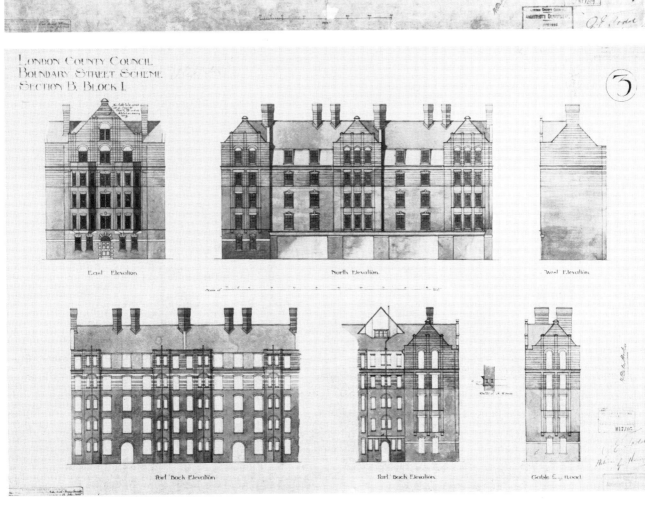

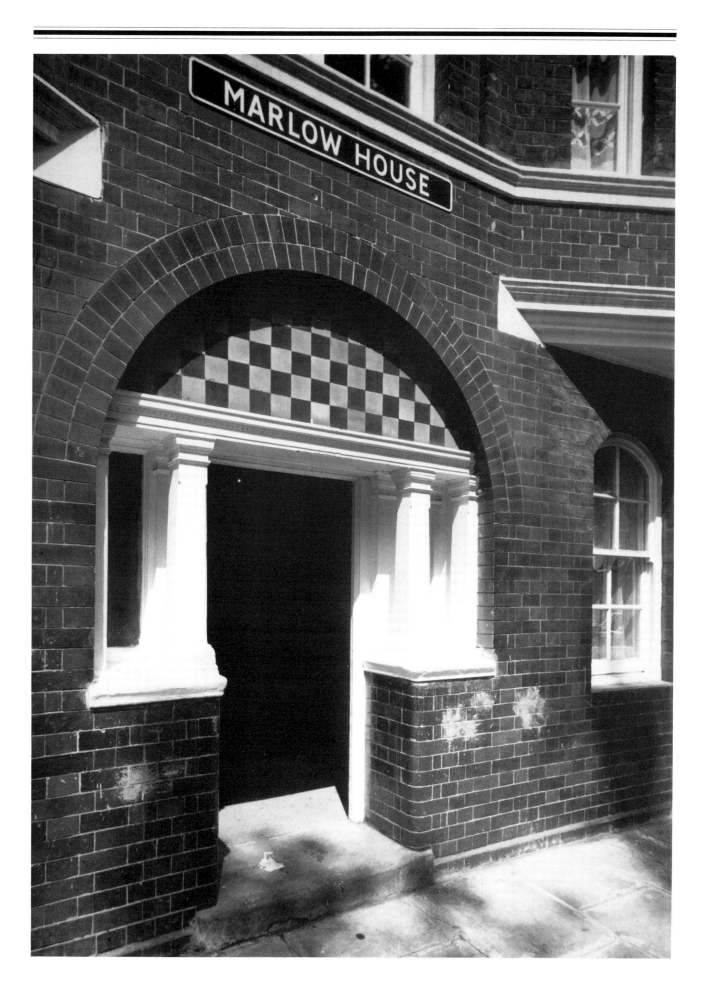

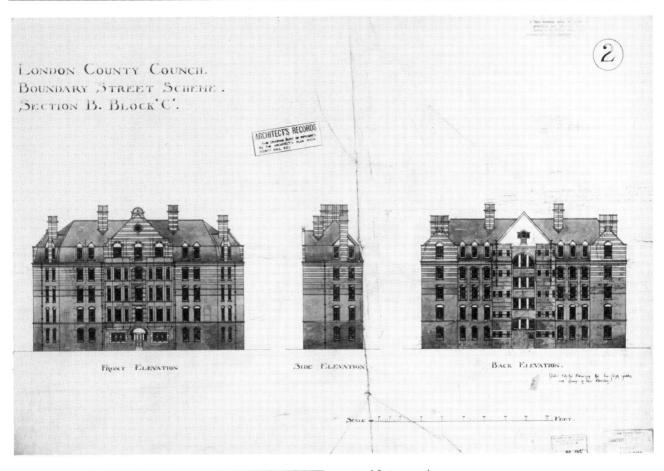

18 (*facing page*)
Marlow House. Detail of entrance from Arnold Circus, echoing that of Shiplake House on the opposite side of Calvert Avenue, the principal approach road.

19 (*above*)
Chertsey House. Elevations. From the original working drawing dated January 1896.

20 (*left*)
Chertsey House. Detail of front elevation and section. From the original working drawing dated January 1896.

21 (*overleaf, left*)
Chertsey House. Detail of rear elevation and section through staircase. From the original working drawing dated January 1896.

22 (*overleaf, right*)
Chertsey House. View from the courtyard.

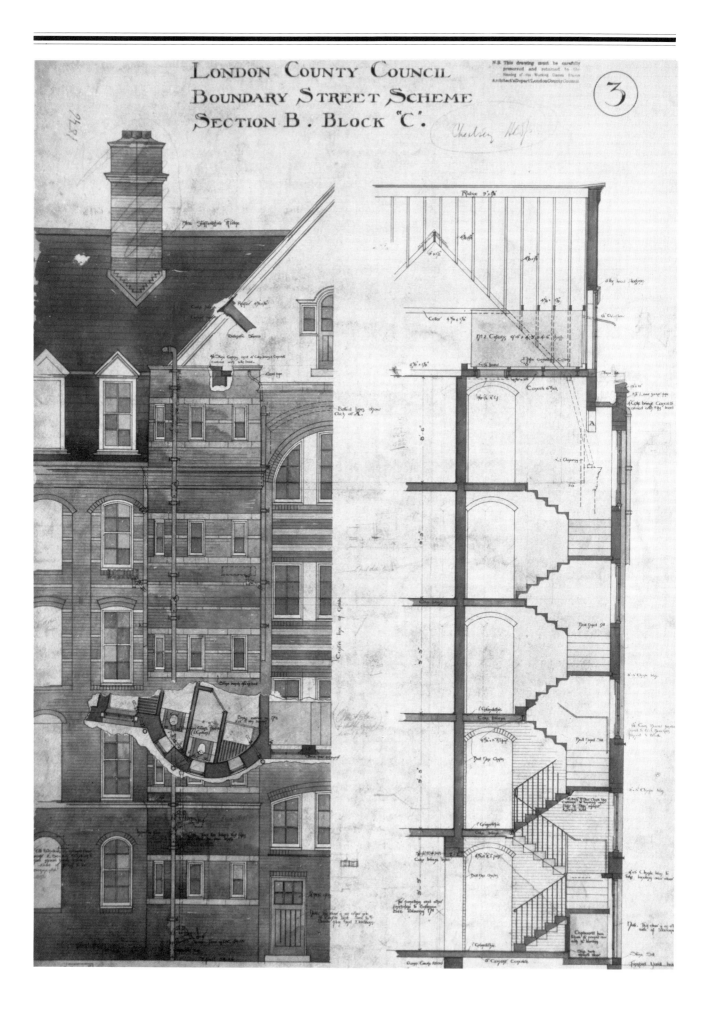

constantly employed by the speculative builder in practising everything bad in building, become utterly demoralised and unfitted to take part in good work. If we are ever to have good Art in common buildings – that is to say, if the housing of the poor is ever to be done by architects and from careful plans and designs – architects themselves must be content to descend frequently from their lofty pedestals, and speak, think and work in simpler phrase. They must learn more of the manner and quality of building, be scrupulously careful about the colour and quality of brickwork, the appearance of its joints, the proper methods to be followed in carpenter's and joiner's work and a thousand other despised things. They must educate the workmen who come within their reach. To do ordinary building well, using every material rightly and truthfully, is the first mark of that interdependence between building and architecture which renders the higher and more intellectual efforts of the latter at all possible. . . . Architecture is not mere display, it is not fashion, and it is not for the rich alone'.[36]

First to be completed, Taylor's Circus blocks were the first to attract the attention of the professional journals though the architectural press, most surprisingly, was never to show a more than cursory interest in the archi-

tectural aspects of the LCC's pioneering housing programme. The equivocal nature of its response is well illustrated by *The British Architect* which gave the Boundary Street scheme unusually good coverage in 1897. 'The London County Council', ran the first report in February, 'for some years past have been devoting the energies of their staff to the preparation of a grand scheme for the re-housing of the working classes. A site near Shoreditch Church was selected for this purpose, and the Boundary Street Working Class Dwellings are well worth visiting now. . . . The plan is that of a great circus, in the middle of which, on an elevated plateau, there is to be a bandstand. Round and about this band-stand come wonderful

23 (*facing page, top*)
Bonner Primary School, Bonner Street, Tower Hamlets. Designed for the London School Board by E R Robson, 1875.
24 (*facing page, bottom*)
Lawrence School, Mansford Street, Tower Hamlets. Designed for the London School Board by E R Robson, 1881.
25 (*above*)
Nos. 126–129 Mount Street, Westminster. Designed by W H Powell, 1886. From The Building News, *17 September 1886.*

'hanging gardens' of *Virginia creepers* and we believe that the 'keep the grass' committee are very pleased with themselves about this piece of artistry. . . . The block [illustrated, a view of Sandford Buildings] is planned with three-roomed tenements, admirably lighted, artistically painted and usefully fitted with 'penny-in-the-slot' meters. In fact, an artist has given orders for his house in Park Lane to be let, and intends to take up his residence here shortly and give art 'At Homes', etc., with notes on the invitation cards that you are respectfully requested to turn up in a costume that will match the paint. In our next 'Street Study' we intend still further illustrating 'Stripeland'. The elevations are worked out as follows: the ground-floor storey is faced with a brown-red salt-glazed brick, and above in red brick striped with a yellow buff ditto, a slate roof finishing the whole'.[37]

Entertaining as Taylor's six early blocks are, they lack the keen originality that he and his colleagues achieved when they broke further away from Shaw's influence and discovered through the work of Philip Webb, avowed seeker after 'commonplace' design, that, as Robson had promised, the same humane and practical architectural vocabulary used with austerity could perfectly express their own radical ideals. Taylor's finest contribution to Boundary Street is Cookham House[38] of 1897 on the south-east corner of the estate, whose elegance is dependent on proportion and an exquisite balance between sculptural and linear form (Plates 26–27). The design was evidently recognised by the Housing branch as one of the

most successful on the estate for it was re-used within a few months as the high point of the Council's next major estate development at Millbank (see page 54). Its significance as the keynote of both schemes was not overlooked by Hermann Muthesius, renowned first historian of the revival of English domestic architecture in the late 19th century. A photograph of the east front of Cookham House is among the illustrations to *Das Englische Haus*, published in 1904, in which Muthesius extols the unique architectural quality of the Council's housing work.[39] No other LCC building is illustrated in the book.

Reginald Minton Taylor, great-grandson of Thomas Minton the founder of the potteries, was born in the same year as Owen Fleming, 1867. From 1884 he spent three years as a pupil and one year as an improver in the office of Peter Paul Pugin, moving on in 1888 to become an assistant to William Wallace (of Wallace and Flockhart), to C H Shoppee, and from 1890 to 1892 to William Young, architect to Lord Cadogan and Lord Wemyss and responsible for many grandiose country houses of the aristocracy. In an early background that sheds little light on Taylor's later development as a designer, only one fact stands out as particularly significant – that he made a special study

26 (*top left*)
Cookham House. Front (east) elevation to Montclare Street.
27 (*top right*)
Cookham House. Rear elevation to courtyard.

during the 1880s of the brick architecture of Holland and eastern England.[40] He joined the staff of the LCC in 1892 and was rapidly promoted within the Housing branch till 1901 when he became a senior officer. Transferred in 1902 to General section he remained there until 1914. After war service he returned to Housing, became head of the section and retired in 1932.[41] He remains an enigmatic figure. Very little is known of his life and opinions, or of the principal early influences upon him, beyond what can be deduced from the buildings that may be tentatively identified as his. It is significant, however, that W R Lethaby was one of the signatories to his application for licentiate membership of the RIBA in 1911. (W E Riley and Harry Redfern were the others). He joined the SPAB in 1907 and the Art Workers' Guild in 1925. Taylor shared with Blashill and many of his fellow architects in Housing a wry disrespect for the public criticism that hounded the Council's every action. He wrote a short article for the staff magazine in 1908 on the Marble Arch Improvement Scheme in which he expressed amazement that traffic conditions at the Arch were 'one of the few, the very few, things (he had) not heard the 'Cahnty Cahncil' abused for' and supposed that 'this trifling omission on the part of our good friend the Man in the Street will be duly rectified when the present improvement is completed'.[42]

While Taylor dominates the architectural character of the northern section of the Boundary Street Estate, the designer whose influence presides over the south was Charles Canning Winmill. Winmill seems to have been largely responsible for the four blocks that flank Club Row, Camlet Street and Ligonier Street: that is, Molesey (1896), Clifton (1897) Laleham and Hedsor Houses (1898), the two last being variations on the same design. He is the best-known member of the group, being the best recorded. The biography written by his daughter in 1937 supplies exactly the kind of personal documentation that is needed to balance the dry official records that are too often the LCC architects' principal memorial.

Winmill was born in 1865. From 1884 to 1888 he was articled to J J Newman FRIBA, from whom, he told Owen Fleming, 'I learnt the values of accuracy and thoroughness'.[43] In 1885 he began attending the design classes of the AA where he met Fleming for the first time. An active member of the Association, he served on the committee of its newly formed Cycling Club in 1887. In the same year, when the publication of *AA Notes* began, he and Fleming were elected Honorary Treasurer and Honorary Secretary respectively. It was during one of the AA's architectural outings in the late 1880s that Winmill first encountered a building by Philip Webb, who became to him, as to most of the group, a fountainhead of inspiration (Plate 28). 'I can never forget my first sight of Joldwynds', he wrote long afterwards to Sydney Cockerell, 'it was practically as the photo in Lethaby's *Philip Webb*: the photo was taken by me some years later. I said to myself: "So architecture does still exist." It took me some years to

get introduced to Philip Webb, as no one in my set knew him. How good to me Philip Webb was, you know well, and of his influence on my life and outlook.'[44] Joyce Winmill recalls that it was her father's habit to declare, 'Anything I know of architecture is due to Philip Webb'. His early designs show, however, that not a little of his architectural knowledge stemmed from his association with Leonard Stokes whose office, at that time in Spring Gardens near the old County Hall, he entered as an assistant early in 1888. Stokes, whose best works rank among the masterpieces of the Arts and Crafts movement, was at that time entering upon the most important stage of his development, abandoning the Gothic idiom of the early '80s for radically simplified compositions based upon an interaction of boldly stressed horizontals and verticals. When Winmill joined the office he was put to work on the designs for the church of St Clare at Sefton Park, Liverpool, and Boxwood Court, Herefordshire.[45] Stokes's house for Wilfred Meynell at Palace Court, Bayswater, was also on the drawing board at that time and seems to have made a powerful impression upon the young man (Plate 29). The 'cultivated mannerism'[46] that Goodhart-Rendel perceived in Stokes's buildings was to haunt Winmill's memory: the wit and originality that illumine his designs for the LCC are its direct descendants. The strong relationship between the work of master and pupil is evident even in Winmill's early schemes produced at AA design classes, such as his projected village church (Plate 30) with the broadly-based stumpy forms and colourful use of materials that are recurring features of Stokes's own style. Winmill's loving description of the tiles he would use for the church is full of an Arts and Crafts fervour. 'The roofs', he noted, 'to be covered with hand-made tiles (like those one sees on St John's, Cambridge. These, I am told, can still be obtained, and weather in from six to ten years to nearly every colour – reds, blues, yellows, browns in many tones – in a way that to me is most delightful), with lead ridge and flashings showing'.[47] The association of Stokes and Winmill, though not always serene, lasted until 1892 'to the great benefit of architecture'. Meanwhile, as Owen Fleming recalled, 'greater events were slowly shaping themselves in the domain of local government'. When it became clear that the policy of the new LCC under the Chairmanship of the Earl of Rosebery, was to be 'creative and enlightened' and the Boundary Street Estate was conceived, 'Winmill joined the group of young architects at work on this scheme and rendered yeoman service in charge of one of the groups of buildings'.[48]

The extent of Winmill's work for Boundary Street is impossible to establish precisely. That he was largely responsible for Molesey, Clifton, Laleham and Hedsor Houses is unarguable, but he made claim, in his declaration for Licentiateship of the RIBA in 1911, to 'eight large blocks of Dwellings, Boundary Street'. Now his initials as examining officer are present on some – but by no means the majority – of the contract drawings for each of the

28 (above)
Joldwynds, Surrey. Designed by Philip Webb, 1872-4.
(Demolished.)
29 (left)
47 Palace Court, Bayswater, Westminster. Designed by
Leonard Stokes, 1888.
30 (facing page)
Design for a Village Church, C C Winmill, 1891. From AA
Notes, *April 1892.*

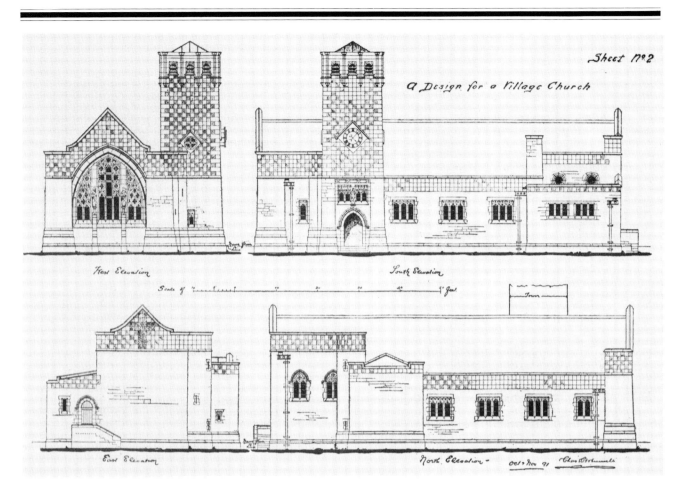

following additional four job groups: Sonning, Culham, Taplow and Sunbury Houses, all in the north-east corner of the estate; it is probable, therefore, that these and the four blocks previously listed make up the eight to which his declaration refers. Sonning and Culham, a pair dating from 1894–5, plain and unremarkable, are difficult to accept as Winmill's designs though their early date may account for their unadventurous external appearance. Yet both were the subject of an accolade – rare for the buildings of Boundary Street – from the contemporary press. 'Architecturally it will probably be one of the best of the dwellings', wrote *The British Architect* of Culham House (Plates 31–32): 'There is apparent more restraint in the design [more, the journal implied, than in the blocks round the central gardens] and generally we like it better – certainly than the blocks immediately opposite [the two blocks, that is, of Streatley Buildings, now demolished, on the other side of Swanfield Street]; these would do very well as infirmary pavilions, and in fact, are suggestive in appearance of microbe propagation – we should not like to live in one of these. The elevations we have illustrated are in yellow stock, striped and varied with red brick and finished with a slate roof'.[49]

Later, the same journal went on to praise Sonning House for its similar merits: 'It is pleasant to find such careful and thoughtful work in a position where one expects only material evidence of plumbers' craft, and windows that suggest at once the usefulness of a small interior chamber. . . .

This court . . . with its overhanging bays, quaint doorways and stripes is quite nice. We should mention that the sanitary work is most excellent throughout the blocks, and might be accepted as a model by many speculating builders. We like very much the good solid base of red brickwork and the plain yellow stocks above, enlivened with the red of the stripes. (Sonning House) . . . in its absolute simplicity and restraint is the type of what we should be glad to see more of'[50] (Plate 33).

Taplow and Sunbury of 1895 and 1896 contain many marks of Winmill's innovations. Even the working drawings for them have a special quality, stylishly executed with clear cool colours, and containing such valuable clues to the Housing branch's tastes as the instruction for a decorated rainwater head to be 'No. 65' from the catalogues of a notable Arts and Crafts metalworker, Thomas Elsley (Plate 34). There is, in all Winmill's designs, a heightened feeling for wall planes, for quality of materials and craftsmanship that derives from the architecture of Philip Webb. The courtyard elevation of Sunbury House, for example (Plate 35), invites comparison with Webb's 35 Glebe Place, Chelsea, a house with which the whole Housing branch must have been familiar (Plate 36). Built of brick on a cramped and narrow site, its segmental-headed sash openings are set, like those of Sunbury, in shallow arched or rectangular recessed panels, neither they nor the doorway with its subtle mouldings disrupting the stern integrity of the wall surface. Tall chimneys punctuate and

31   (above)
Culham House. Front elevation to garden.
32   (facing page)
Culham House. Rear elevation to courtyard.
33   (left)
Sonning House. Rear elevation to Mount Street.

34   (overleaf, left)
Sunbury House. Detail of courtyard elevation. From the original working drawing dated 1895.
35   (overleaf, right)
Sunbury House. Courtyard elevation.

36 (*left*)
35 *Glebe Place, Chelsea. Designed by Philip Webb, 1869.*
37 (*below*)
Clifton House. Elevation to Club Row (formerly Ainsworth Street). From the original drawing dated March 1897.
38 (*bottom*)
Clifton House. Courtyard elevation. From the original working drawing dated March 1897.
39 (*facing page*)
1 Holland Park Road, Kensington. Elevations. Designed by Philip Webb, 1864–5 with additions 1892. From the contract drawing in the RIBA Drawings Collection.

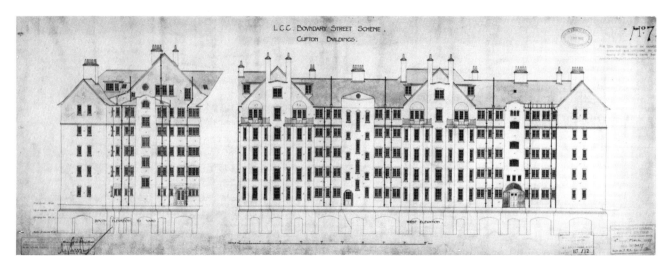

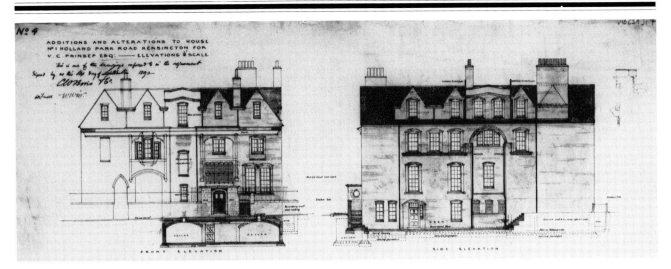

emphasise the irregularity of the plan and the roofline which dips and rises and projects as if to suggest slow and natural growth, an impression reinforced by the calculated asymmetry of the elevation. This stylistic device on which the whole of the vernacular revival had been based was to be seized upon by the Housing branch as a weapon in the campaign against the double standard for it stood for all those concepts – of privacy and the changing needs of the individual, of haphazard growth and comfortable informality – that had been harshly denied by the housing trusts and for which the very slums were still mourned by many of those who had been rehoused.

Clifton House of 1897 is probably Winmill's most inspired contribution to Boundary Street, though he was to recall long afterwards that he had protested when Owen Fleming asked him to prepare plans for it in July: 'No one should be pressed to design this time of year'.[51] It shows how Webb's architectural vocabulary was adapted to suit the requirements of the large block dwelling, a building type for which, it must be remembered, neither Webb nor Lethaby, for all their dreams and aspirations, could offer a precedent (Plates 37–41). The effect of busy variety and growth is more striking on site than might be supposed from the drawings, for Clifton House is wrapped about the outline of its site to form a comfortable enclosure with Molesey House on the west (Plates 42–44). Colour was evidently of the utmost importance to Winmill and to the branch in general – many of the drawings are a feast to the eye – though it had to be introduced simply and cheaply, relying heavily on the use of white and the natural colour of materials: red bricks, glazed and unglazed, and the darker red of roof tiles, chequered and glazed tile patterns, white sashes and white cement-rendered or rough-cast gables, attics and entrance porches, the attics striped by contrasting balcony grilles. A comparison of the courtyard doorways at Clifton House and Laleham House with those on the Guinness Estate of similar date nearby describes more eloquently than any words the gulf that separates their respective architects' approach to working class housing (Plates 45–48). The element of humour and surprise in Winmill's designs, as

in the capping of a cylindrical staircase tower on Laleham House with the same triangular form used for the flat projection (Plates 49–50), his evident delight in pure geometrical forms and in exploiting their sculptural qualities, make his the most exciting of all the blocks of dwellings on the Boundary Street Estate, and set them in the same line of development as the works in the 1890s of Leonard Stokes and Harrison Townsend. In 1900 Winmill was transferred to the Fire Brigade branch. He remained there until he retired from the Council's service and returned to private practice in 1923. He died in 1945.

Wargrave House of 1897 and Benson House of 1898, two of the four blocks that complete the south-west corner of the estate, appear to have been in the special charge of William Hynam by whom most of their drawings are initialled. Little is known of this architect and his handling of the elevations suggests that, while he was an able interpreter of the group's house-style, he had little original contribution to make to its development (Plates 51–52). He was born in 1869 and became a member of the Architectural Association in 1887, attending the design classes there before joining the staff of the Architect's Department in 1892.[41] In 1912 he was elected a Licentiate of the RIBA but the declaration papers that might provide much-needed details of his early life and training have not yet come to light. He remained with the Housing branch for the rest of his career and retired in 1924. The *LCC Staff Gazette* wrote that he came 'of architectural stock and, as a consequence, at the age of twenty-three, was already extraordinarily well informed, not only as regards construction, but also in sanitary science, in which indeed his knowledge was remarkable. In those early days there was no departmental tradition to go upon; each had to set his own course and to make his own chart'.[52] The working drawings for the laundry at Boundary Street, dated 1895, are all initialled

40 (*overleaf, left*)
Clifton House. View in courtyard looking north.
41 (*overleaf, right*)
Clifton House. View in courtyard looking south.

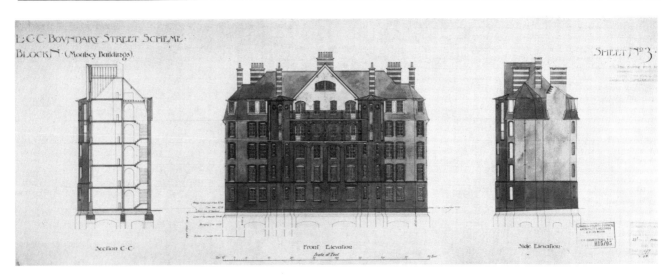

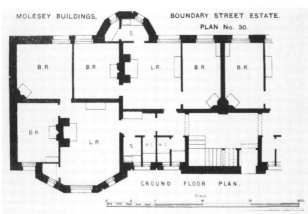

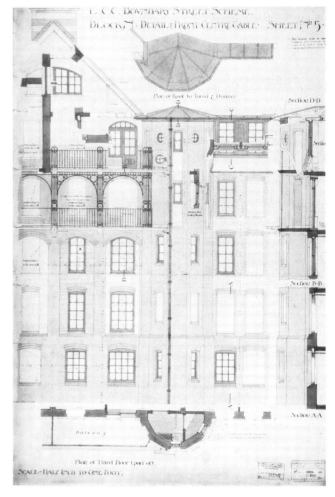

42 (top)
Molesey House. Front and side elevations and section. From the original working drawing dated October 1896.

43 (above)
Molesey House. Ground floor plan, showing a variation of the associated type with private WC and some of the sculleries set outside the flats on the communal hallways.

44 (right)
Molesey House. Detail of front elevation. From the original working drawing dated October 1896.

45 (facing page, top left)
Clifton House. A courtyard entrance.

46 (facing page, top right)
Clifton House. A courtyard entrance.

47 (facing page, bottom left)
Guinness Trust Estate, Columbia Road, Tower Hamlets. A courtyard entrance.

48 (facing page, bottom right)
Laleham House. A courtyard entrance.

49 (top)
Laleham House. View in the courtyard. From the sketch by Raffles Davison published in the RIBA Journal 7 April 1900.
50 (left)
Laleham House. Detail of a staircase tower.
51 (facing page)
Benson House. Elevations and section. From the original working drawing dated June 1898.
52 (above)
Benson House. Detail of front elevation.

by Hynam as examining officer (Plate 53). 'A dignified little block', pronounced *The British Architect*, drawing attention also to its possible social benefits as a meeting place for residents, 'The only fault we can find is the doorway – this is abominable'.[53]

Iffley House and Abingdon House of 1896 and 1898 were, on firm evidence, the responsibility of A M Philips, a very much better-documented figure whose powers as a designer are worth special attention. Arthur Maxwell Philips was born in 1868 and went to Kensington Grammar and Merchant Taylors School.[54] From 1886 to 1889 he served his articles with J J Stevenson, one-time partner of E R Robson, School Board architect, and, like him, able champion of the red-brick Queen Anne style which he saw as the means of achieving a vigorous modern architecture. When Philips joined the Council's staff he established a direct link between the Housing branch and Stevenson's clear-cut ideas on the nature of materials, on economy of means, proportion and functionalism, though in their published form these ideas would already have been known to his colleagues there.[55] There was much to be said for the new style on practical grounds, Stevenson had declared in 1874. 'Take the ordinary conditions of London building – stock bricks and sliding sash windows. A flat arch of red cut bricks is the cheapest mode of forming the window-head: the red colour is naturally carried down the sides of the window, forming a frame; and is used also to emphasise the angles of the building.

As the gables rise above the roofs it costs nothing, and gives interest and character . . . to mould them into curves and sweeps. The appearance of wall-surface carried over the openings, which, in Gothic, the tracery and iron bars and reflecting surface of thick stained glass had taught us to appreciate, is obtained by massive wooden frames and sash bars set, where the silly interference of the Building Act does not prevent, almost flush with the walls; while the rooms inside these thick sash bars give a feeling of enclosure and comfort. With these simple elements the style is complete, without any expenditure whatever on ornament. . . . There is nothing but harmony and proportion to depend on for effect. . . . The style in all its forms has the merit of truthfulness; it is the outcome of our common modern wants picturesquely expressed. In its mode of working and details it is the common vernacular style in which the British workman has been apprenticed. . . .'.[56]

In 1888 while in Stevenson's office Philips joined the AA and there met – probably for the first time – Owen Fleming and Charles Winmill. In 1889 he became an assistant to Herbert Read and Robert MacDonald. MacDonald himself was a former pupil of Stevenson and the partners had worked together in the office of Ernest George before setting up in practice. Their London work is a well-mannered fusion of Queen Anne and the more sober elements of George's exotic Northern Renaissance revivalism. To Philips their office must have seemed a

natural progression from his training with Stevenson and he remained with the firm until 1891. After a brief period with F W Troup he went in 1892 to spend about a year as assistant to J M Brydon, architect of Chelsea Town Hall (1885), close friend of Leonard Stokes (who later extended the Town Hall on the King's Road front) and among the first to revive the English Baroque manner. Major schemes upon which Philips worked for Brydon included Chelsea Polytechnic and Bath Municipal Buildings. In January 1893 he joined the Housing branch as a temporary assistant at £2. 12s. 6d a week.[41] On the occasion of his application to become a Licentiate of the RIBA in 1911, Philips troubled to list in much greater detail than was usual the works he had undertaken for the LCC. They are described as follows: 'Drawings for the Working Classes at West View Estate Greenwich (£24,000), Hughes Fields Deptford (£32,000), Idenden Cottages, Greenwich (£16,000), Southwark Dwellings, Green Street and Gun Street (£19,000), Iffley and Abingdon Buildings, Boundary Street Estate (£30,000). The working drawings were made and the supervision of the drawings on the following estates conducted in the sub-section of the Housing of the Working Classes Section entrusted to my direction: 4 buildings on the Millbank Estate, the Totterdown Fields, the Norbury, the White Hart Lane Estates, the lay-out of the Millbank Estate.'[54]

Winmill wrote that 'Philips's architectural capacity can

be judged from the work he was mainly responsible for, such as Iddenden [sic] Cottages, East Greenwich'[57] (see page 85). It is interesting that he should have singled out the cottages, now demolished, for though they were by no means the most original of Philips's works they fore-shadowed the Council's later cottage estates, the area in which Philips seems to have exerted most influence and in which he undoubtedly felt most at ease. Iffley House is conspicuous among the blocks fronting onto the Circus as the only one with ponderous classical motifs echoing Brydon's neo-Baroque style (Plate 54), while at Abingdon House the details sit awkwardly on the massive façades as if they ought to belong to some much smaller building (Plates 55–56).

Philips's masterpiece of block design is a small low-rise estate of four three-storeyed tenements – that listed by him as the Green Street and Gun Street (now Rushworth Street and Boyfield Street) scheme, Southwark. Plans for Merrow, Ripley, Albury and Clandon Houses were ready early in 1896 and the dwellings were completed by the Council's Works Department and occupied in the summer of 1897 (Plates 57–61). 420 people were provided for, in thirteen one-roomed, seventy-one two-roomed and eighteen three-roomed flats, all self-contained. The two pairs of buildings, identical in all but their grouping, are separated from each other by Webber Street running from east to west. Albury and Clandon face each other

across Boyfield Street, to which each presents a simple balconied elevation. Ripley and Merrow are set back to back, the same balconied elevations forming an intimate courtyard enclosure, while the elevation used for the rear of Albury and Clandon is here given precedence as the front to Rushworth Street and King's Bench Walk respectively. It is a design of the most touching simplicity and refinement, unsurpassed in beauty of proportion and brickwork, in economy and invention of decorative detail, by any public housing scheme of comparable date. While the built designs express an architectural idealism peculiar to the Housing branch, the drawings – especially those for balcony iron-work – reveal how closely the group identified with one of the most widely-shared ideals of the age; the unity of craftsmanship and art. Close by Philips's scheme, on the Borough Road Estate developed by the LCC four years later, stand Murphy, Hunter and Gardner Buildings, examples of the Council's unfortunate urge to speed up the housing programme by employing outside architects (Plate 62). These are the work of Joseph, Son and Smithem, well-known in their day as designers of block dwellings for the working classes. The contrast between Rushworth Street or the Boundary Estate and these lofty flats, drab and ill-defined despite their smattering of terra-cotta decoration and elaborately gabled and panelled staircase bays, shows how far the Housing architects had already progressed by 1897 in their revolt against received

53 (*facing page, left*)
Central Laundry. Detail of front elevation. From the original working drawing dated July 1895.
54 (*facing page, right*)
Iffley House. Front elevation to Arnold Circus.
55 (*top*)
Abingdon House. Elevation to Navarre Street.
56 (*above*)
Abingdon House. Detail of courtyard elevation.

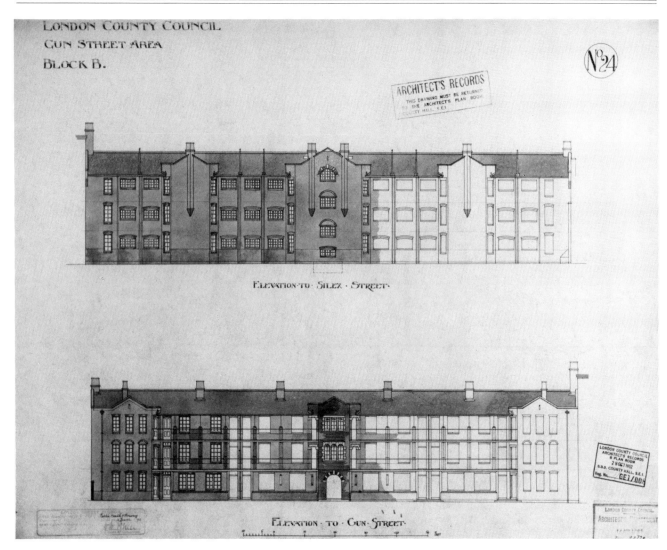

57 (*top*)
'*Green and Gun Street*' *scheme, Southwark. From the original working drawings for Albury and Clandon Houses, dated 1896.*

58 (*left*)
'*Green and Gun Street*' *scheme, Southwark. Ripley and Merrow Houses. Elevation to Kings Bench Walk.*

59 (*facing page, top left*)
Ripley and Merrow Houses. Detail of elevation to Rushworth Street.

60 (*facing page, top right*)
Ripley and Merrow Houses. Detail of courtyard elevation.

61 (*facing page, bottom*)
'*Green and Gun Street*' *scheme. Details of balcony ironwork. From the original drawing dated 1896.*

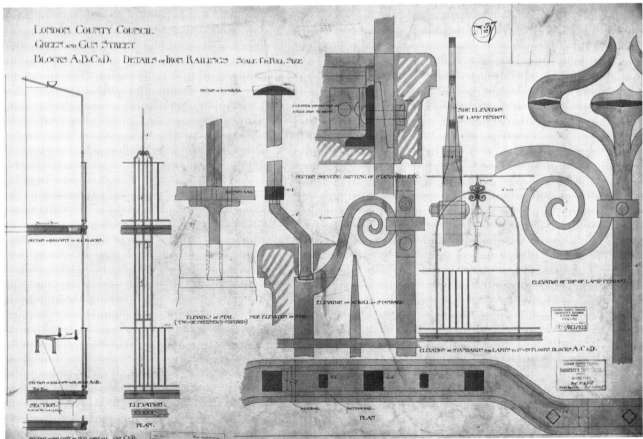

ideas of the 'suitable' working class tenement. It is difficult to understand why the little flatted terraces of Rushworth and Boyfield Street, offering, it now seems, an ideal alternative to the much-hated five-storey 'barrack' dwellings, attracted no special attention at the time of their erection. The Council's housing handbook of 1913 includes a photograph of Joseph and Smithem's Murphy House but none of Ripley, Merrow, Clandon or Albury – an oversight shared by architectural journals at the time and, apparently, by writers on English architecture ever since.

Shortly after the completion of his Southwark dwellings Philips was promoted within the branch to the rank of permanent staff, 2nd class. In April 1899 he was up-graded again and by 1901 was a senior assistant earning £300 a year. Suddenly, in 1907, he was transferred to an administrative section of the Department dealing with means of escape from buildings in case of fire, where his skills as a designer would have had no outlet at all.[41] 'His friends', Charles Winmill was to record, 'felt that it was a slur on his capacity that he should have been transferred from the Housing Section to purely routine work, one never heard any complaint from him for that official action'.[57] In the same year Philips and his former colleague in Housing, Reginald Minton Taylor, joined the SPAB where

he sat on the committee with Winmill, Webb, Lethaby, Thackeray Turner and his former master J J Stevenson and 'seldom missed attending the weekly meetings'. As a member of the National Reserve and one time Captain in the 17th Middlesex Rifles, he joined up immediately when war began and was killed in action at Gallipoli in November 1915 at the age of 47.[58]

That it would be wrong to try to divide responsibility for design at Boundary Street neatly among the officers who signed the drawings is shown by the conspicuous absence from the signatories, not only of Owen Fleming, the group leader, but of T G Charlton and Robert Robertson his two chief assistants. Both were, like Fleming, Winmill, Philips and Hynam, AA members and students: they joined in 1889 and 1891 respectively. Thomas Gardhouse Charlton was born in Carlisle in 1868 and served his articles with a local architect, C J Ferguson, from 1884 to 1889. After a brief period in a Leeds office he came in 1891 to London 'and studied in the Architectural

62 (*above*)
Murphy House, Borough Road Estate, Southwark. Designed by Joseph, Son and Smithem, 1900.

Atelier, Heddon Street, the AA Classes, the Royal Academy schools and occasionally doing work for architects in practice'.[59] In 1892 he was elected Associate of the RIBA. Leonard Stokes was one of his sponsors. 'Mr Charlton', recorded his obituary in a Carlisle newspaper, 'performed important work as the Chief Assistant in the housing branch of the LCC . . . (At Boundary Street) he acted as resident architect during the initial stages and until the erection of dwellings was fairly on their way. After being with the LCC for six years [sic, but he did not resign until early in 1898] he started in private practice in the City of London but on the death of his father he disposed of his London practice and came to reside in Carlisle'.[60] He died in 1935.

'Rob' Robertson, born in 1866 in Scotland, was educated at Edinburgh School of Art and articled to the Edinburgh architect J Russell Walker. He spent a brief period as assistant in George Baines's City of London office before joining the staff of the LCC. On his Licentiate's declaration form submitted to the RIBA in 1911 he noted, 'Have taken a leading part in designing all the large Housing Schemes for the LCC – for example – Boundary Street area, Millbank area, Caledonian Estate, White Hart Lane, Tottenham (Garden Suburb), Norbury Estate, Totterdown Fields Estate, Old Oak Lane Estate (Garden Suburb)'. Again Stokes was one of his sponsors. W E Riley, another, stated that he had known the candidate from 1899 and that 'during the whole of this period he has carried out under my direction many architectural works which are above the scale of importance met with in many cases of private practice'.[61] Robertson was appointed head of Housing branch in 1901 and in 1910 was transferred to Schools division. Shortly before his death in 1939 he set up in private practice.[62]

The Boundary Street Estate, largest yet attempted under the Housing of the Working Classes Act of 1890, was formally opened on 3 March 1900 by the Prince of Wales, who professed himself to be 'greatly pleased with the design of the buildings'.[63] Calculated on the basis of two people to a room, provision had been made for the re-housing of 5,380 people in 1,069 flats. These varied widely in size and type. Fifteen were of one room only, 541 of two rooms, 103 of four rooms, seven of five rooms, and three of six rooms. Of these 601 were fully self-contained, 201 self-contained with detached but private lavatories, ninety had private lavatories and sculleries outside on the landing, 142 had private lavatories outside but shared a scullery and only thirty-five, of which fifteen were one-roomed flats concentrated in Culham House, were entirely on the associated plan, sharing both lavatories and sculleries with other tenants. During the first stage of the development of Boundary Street the average size of living rooms was 144 square feet and of bedrooms 96 square feet though in later buildings these dimensions were increased to 160 and 110. 'Every habitable room on the area is provided with a 45° angle of light horizontally and vertically. The buildings are so arranged that nearly every room commands a pleasant outlook'.[64] The whole endeavour had cost the Council well over £600,000. 'The sum expended is undoubtedly large', said the Prince of Wales at the opening ceremony, 'but not large in proportion to the benefits which are secured; for, instead of some thousands of persons living under grave insanitary conditions, dying at the rate of which we have been told, breeding disease, which is not only prejudicial to themselves, but which constitutes a danger to the whole of London, we have a population of almost the same size living under conditions which are in every way favourable to health and comfort'.[65] In April Blashill, responding to Owen Fleming's paper on the Estate read at the RIBA, took the opportunity to make a last public statement on the subject of Boundary Street. He referred 'in eulogistic terms' to the staff who had been engaged on the scheme. 'Every one of them had contributed to the success of the work, and deserved a full share of whatever credit attached to it. With so little variety of materials – with nothing more ornamental than great bands of brickwork, which was all they could afford – it must be acknowledged that they had achieved, from an architectural point of view, very satisfactory results'. But he could not resist commenting a little acidly on the idealistic attitudes that had exacerbated the difficulties of his task. No class of society, he protested, could have houses perfect in every respect, yet it had been driven home to them at every turn that in an artisan's dwelling everything *must* be perfect: 'The philanthropist would listen to no economies where provision had to be made for the labouring classes. Yet to have cheaper buildings we must economise in every way'. A member of the County Council had once protested to him, he recalled, against the cruelty of having no lifts in an artisan's dwelling of five storeys high – 'it was "too bad", he said, "to make them climb so high"'.[66]

Sentiment jostled with cynicism in the architectural profession's reaction to the social phenomenon of Boundary Street: one critic wrote in *AA Notes* of the decline of LCC ideals in creating such high-density housing, 'and to make matters worse the Council must needs make an artificial mountain of rubbish and excavation debris, piled as high as the first floor in the central open space, so as to impede, effectually, the free passage of such air as there is in that quarter. . . .' Tenements should be airy and sunny, he declared, outlining his own vision of balconies 'into which the inmates may step out even into the open, and where a few creepers, flowers, mignonette, and a little thyme, rosemary and even perhaps the sweet English rose may be made to grow in boxes and pots, all of which, at little cost, will minister, by their fragrance and beauty, to the joy and comfort of the dwellers. . . .'[67] *The British Architect*, on the other hand, one of the few journals to have commented favourably on the design and planning of the estate, considered the amenities overdone: 'The fortunate craftsmen who take up their abode here will, from the bay windows . . . command the bandstand, the hanging gardens of virginian creepers and all the other delights of this workman's paradise. In the evening at dinner, work over for the day, that pampered pet, the British workman, will no doubt speculate as to how long it will be before the Government not only educate him free of charge and house him for next door to the same thing, but when they really mean to allow him to pass from the partly useful to the wholly ornamental. . . . '.[68]

Social commentators were equally grudging in their acknowledgement of what the LCC had achieved and the most vehement criticism was that the needs of the very poor had been ignored altogether. 'It is a mistake', said John Honeyman at the RIBA in 1900, 'to praise the LCC . . . for erecting artisans' dwellings, while they do absolutely nothing towards providing suitable dwellings for the poorest class.'[69] Yet the decision to provide dwellings for a section of the working class somewhat above the poorest had not been taken lightly. Giving evidence before the 1884 Royal Commission on the housing question Octavia Hill had advised that there was a group comprised principally of the 'criminal and destructive class' that 'cannot be dealt with by the existing or by any other building societies' and for which a different system of housing would have to be arranged. The Council, anxious to raise and not merely to maintain existing standards, had resolved to act by this advice.[70] Charles Booth admitted that 'in designing these buildings trouble was taken to suit them to the special needs of the displaced peoples, room being provided for costers' barrows and workshops for cabinet-makers and others; while the rents were put as low as would cover working charges, and meet the interest and sinking fund on the money borrowed. But all', he added, 'to no purpose. The various expenses incurred in effecting the clearance had been enormous, and it may be that too much was yielded to the desire to build dwellings that should at once be a credit to the London County Council and an example to others. At any rate, the cost was too great, the rents too high and, in addition, the regulations to be observed under the new conditions, demanded more orderliness of behaviour than suited the old residents. The result is that the new buildings are occupied by a different class, largely Jews, and that the inhabitants of the demolished dwellings have overrun the neighbouring poor streets, or have sought new homes further and further afield, as section after section was turned adrift'.[71] Arthur Morrison put the exodus of the slum population down, not to high rents, but to sheer prejudice against buildings in flats. Having described in *A Child Of the Jago* how 'after long delay the crude yellow brick of the barrack dwellings rose above the oft-stolen hoardings and grew, storey to storey', he ended the book with a final flourish of pessimism: 'the dispossessed Jagos [slum-dwellers] had gone to infect the neighbourhoods across the border, and crowd the people a little closer. They did not return to live in the new barrack-buildings; which was a strange thing, for the County Council was charging very little more than double the rents which the landlords [of the Old Nichol] had charged. And so another

Jago, teeming and villainous as the one displaced, was slowly growing, in the form of a ring, round about the great yellow houses'.[72]

By the time the Boundary Street Estate was opened the Council had already embarked upon its second large flatted housing scheme. Owen Fleming proudly announced at the RIBA in April 1900 that 'The Millbank Estate, which is to West London what Boundary Street is to East London, will be completed probably within two years from the present time. It will house over 4,000 persons, and will be perhaps more sattely in architectural character than Boundary Street could have been'.[73] Laid out in formal grandeur about a garden, on the site of Millbank Penitentiary behind the Tate Gallery, this red-brick estate of five-storey blocks is the branch's crowning achievement under Thomas Blashill's leadership (Plates 63-64). The jewel in the crown, the control block upon which the estate plan depends is a design borrowed from Boundary Street: Hogarth House facing the gardens at the end of St Oswulf Street is Reginald Minton Taylor's Cookham House in reverse, the gabled rear elevation of Cookham used here as the principal front that closes magnificently the central vista from Dundonald Street (Plates 65-70). At Boundary Street variety is the key note of the estate. At Millbank the theme is symmetry. Not only are the blocks laid out symmetrically on either side of Hogarth House and the central garden, but they are arranged so that each is answered on the corresponding side of the central axis by the same design in reverse; thus Turner and Ruskin Buildings on the estate plan are handed blocks, as also are Leighton and Millais, Mulready and Landseer, and so on (Plates 71-73). Only Hogarth is unique, though that too has its counterpart – at Bethnal Green. Seldom can the need for economy – of time and means and skill – have been turned to such brilliant account in an exercise of planning. Though more formal than Boundary Street in both layout and architectural effect, Millbank is as far removed as the East End estate from the bleak monotony of its predecessors. The blocks, though strictly ordered, are wrapped about their plots so as to create, on the ground, a subtle balance between spaciousness and gentle enclosure, between informality on individual plots and the overall 'stateliness' that Fleming had described.

Millbank was planned to accommodate 4,430 people displaced by slum clearance and road improvement schemes within a radius of two miles. The Council stood immovable on its decision to provide housing for a class above the very poorest and despite vociferous demands for more single-roomed dwellings, made provision for precisely two of these at Millbank (in Gainsborough House). No tenements had both WC and scullery in common with others and by far the larger number were entirely self-contained. Hogarth was the first block to be completed. It was built by the Council's Works Department and was ready for occupation in May 1899. Rents ranged from seven shillings to thirteen shillings a week for its fifty-four

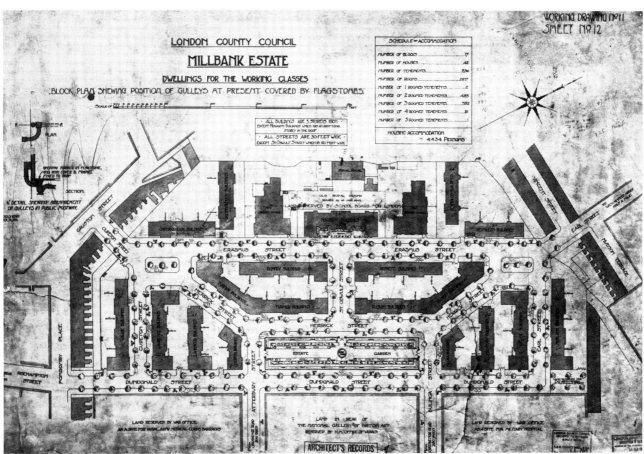

tenements, comprising one unit of five rooms, ten units of four rooms, twenty-two of three rooms and twenty-one of two rooms. Twenty-four of the flats were entirely self-contained and the remaining thirty were self-contained with private lavatories detached. Despite the claims of many, including A M Philips, to have participated in Millbank, its conception must be ascribed to one man only, Reginald Minton Taylor, architect of Hogarth House which summarizes in its immaculate elevations the unique quality of this estate. Taylor was directly responsible also for the working drawings of Leighton and Millais, and Turner and Ruskin which were commenced (by Holloway Bros) immediately after Hogarth in 1898 and 1899. The drawings for Romney (now Stubbs) and Rossetti, dated July 1899 (also built by Holloway) are initialled by a junior draughtsman William Marchment, acting, it may be assumed, for Taylor as Divisional Officer. The Millbank Estate together with its related drawings, was handed over to the City of Westminster on 1st April 1980.

The architecture of Millbank represents the climax of the stylistic relationship between the work of Taylor and his colleagues and that of the architect-members of the SPAB. The Society's Secretary, Thackeray Turner, had built in 1894 at Guildford, a block of flats that foreshadows, to a startling degree, many characteristic features of the LCC house-style (Plate 74). The strong family resemblance between Taylor's Ruskin and Turner Houses at Millbank (Plates 75–76) and Thackeray Turner's fashionable terrace at

Lygon Place, Westminster of 1909–10 (Plate 77) illustrates the cross-fertilization of ideas that was constantly at work within the Arts and Crafts movement. The hooded entrances with their boldly simplified chunky brackets are outstandingly similar, while both elevations are informed by the same restraint and modesty of architectural vocabulary; both display a highly sophisticated use of simple and familiar forms and proportions whilst scrupulously avoiding those stylistic tricks and lifeless formulas so much despised by Lethaby and his disciples.

The homogeneity of style which is, as Taylor intended, crucial to the character of the estate, was seriously threatened when the Council once again raised the question of introducing an outside architect. It was as if the Housing of the Working Classes Committee remained unconvinced that high architectural quality could be compatible with stringent economy. A limited competition was launched in 1897 and the assessor W D Caroe awarded first premium to Spalding and Cross's design for a specimen block. Investigations then began to discover whether their scheme could be carried out, like the blocks already produced by the Housing branch, without incurring a charge on London rates. Happily for Millbank this was found to be impossible, 'and they came to the conclusion

---

63 (*above*)
Block plan of the Millbank Estate, Westminster. From the original working drawing dated 1903.

THE ARCHITECTS OF BOUNDARY STREET AND MILLBANK 57

at the LCC that they had nothing to learn from outside and that their own recognised plan was far ahead of any sent in'.[74] The Architect was instructed forthwith to prepare plans for the remaining ten buildings, Gainsborough (two blocks) and Reynolds (two blocks), Lawrence and Maclise (Plates 78–83) Landseer and Mulready, and Morland and Wilkie. Tenders for all ten were accepted from Messrs Spencer, Santo and Co., in March 1900. Again Reginald Minton Taylor was the guiding force in the design of the blocks. He himself initialled most of the plans for Maclise, handed with Lawrence, and for Landseer, handed with Mulready. The drawings for Wilkie and Morland, dated July 1900, were initialled on his behalf by E P Wheeler, then among the junior draughting staff (and destined to rise to the position of Architect to the Council in 1935). In only one instance does the possibility arise of a significant contribution by another designer: the drawings for Gainsborough House, dated April 1899, bear the initials of Charles Winmill whose hand may be detected in the original and idiosyncratic detailing of the attic storey (Plates 84–85).

The architectural uniformity of Millbank is perhaps the quality which most distinguishes it from Boundary Street. Indeed, the fertility of ideas and sheer enthusiasm for picturesque effects displayed in the earlier scheme have no parallel in the work of the Housing branch. As Thomas Blashill laconically remarked, 'Boundary Street was about as far as they would be able to go' towards architectural variety.[75] As the volume of work steadily increased, so the opportunity for such concentration of skills as steadily diminished. Each estate would now be assigned, like Millbank, to the overall control of one designer. Linked still by the shared experience of Boundary Street, the group continued to draw upon the rich repository of ideas that had been established there. Some of the courtyard entrances at Millbank are remarkable examples of this process of development and refinement. The porches of Maclise and its handed block Lawrence (Plate 83), as dramatic in effect as open-air sculptures, have their starting point in the porch designed by Winmill for Laleham House, little more than a year previously (Plate 48). The breadth and simplicity of their contrasting white planes, stout battered piers and mortar-board caps, the head-long pitch of the silvery-grey slate roofs broken by tiny dormers, reveal an approach to three-dimensional form as colourful and inventive as that of Mackintosh, Smith and Brewer, Harrison Townsend or E S Prior. The Millbank porches express, above all, a joyous determination to apply to council housing the same standard of architectural grace, the same depth of design, that at present benefited only the rich and fashionable.

64 (left)
View of the Millbank Estate looking north. From an LCC photograph taken c 1906.

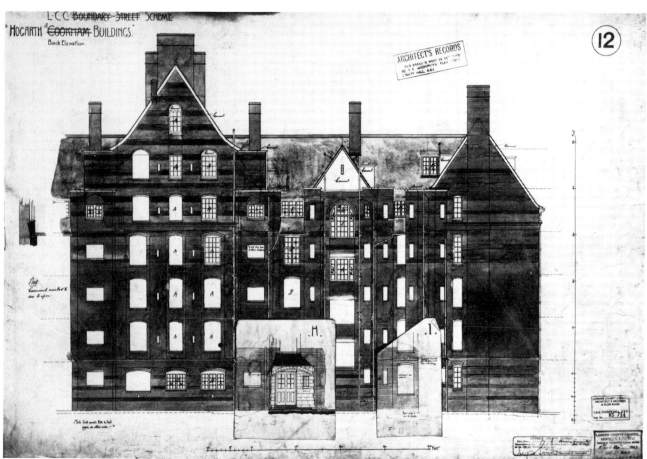

65 (facing page, top)
Hogarth House. From an LCC photograph taken in August 1906.
66 (facing page, bottom)
Hogarth House. Front elevation, adapted from the back elevation of Cookham House, Boundary Street. From the original working drawing dated December 1897, with fly-overs.
67 (left)
Hogarth House. Detail of central gabled bay, principal front.
68 (below)
Hogarth House. Detail of central bay, principal front.

69 (*left*)
Hogarth House. Entrance on principal front.
70 (*below*)
Hogarth House. A living room. From an LCC photograph of 1906.
71 (*facing page, top*)
Handed blocks Leighton and Millais Houses. Front elevation and elevation to Herrick Street. From the original working drawing dated October 1898.
72 (*facing page, bottom*)
Leighton and Millais Houses. Ground floor plan. From The Housing Question in London, *LCC, 1900, p 272.*

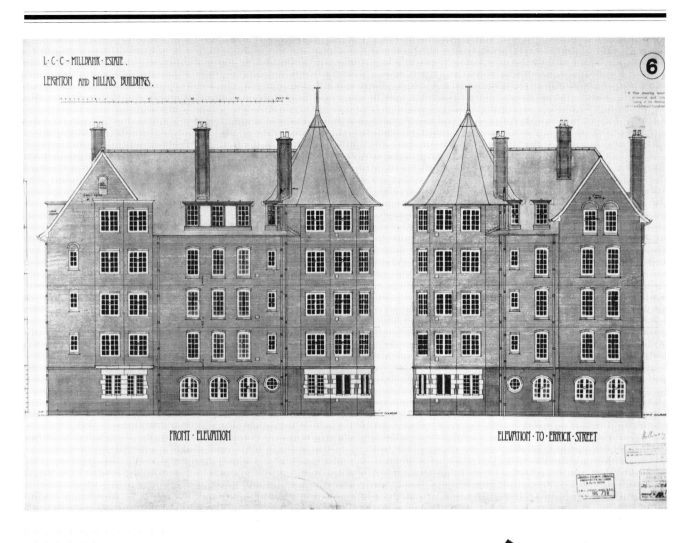

FRONT · ELEVATION ELEVATION · TO · ERRICK · STREET

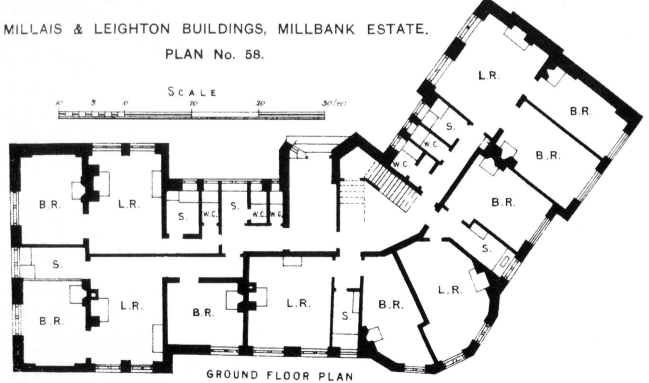

MILLAIS & LEIGHTON BUILDINGS, MILLBANK ESTATE.

PLAN No. 58.

GROUND FLOOR PLAN

73 (*facing page*)
Leighton House. View of principal front from Herrick Street.
74 (*left*)
Wycliffe Buildings, Portsmouth Road, Guildford, Surrey.
Designed by Thackeray Turner, 1894.
75 (*bottom left*)
Turner House. Courtyard elevation from Erasmus Street.
76 (*below*)
Turner House. A courtyard entrance.
77 (*bottom right*)
Lygon Place, Westminster. Designed by Thackeray Turner, 1909.

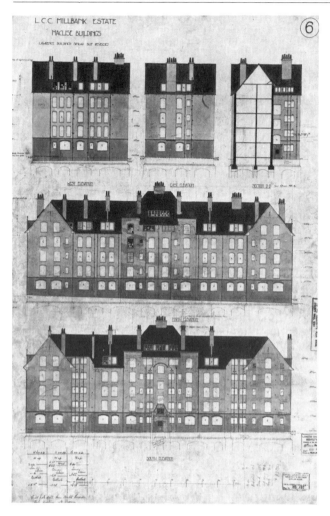

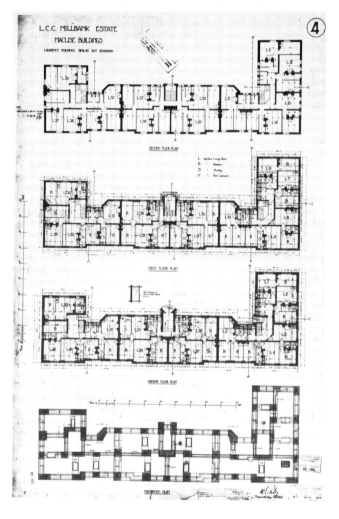

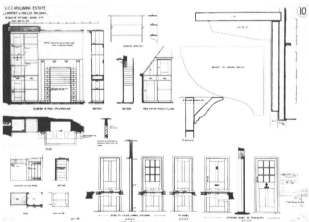

78 (top left)
Handed blocks Lawrence and Maclise. Elevations and section.
From the original working drawing dated October 1901.
79 (top right)
Handed blocks Lawrence and Maclise. Plans. From the
original working drawing dated June 1900.
80 (above)
Handed blocks Lawrence and Maclise. Details of fittings,
doors, etc. From the original working drawing dated June 1900.

81 (facing page)
Handed blocks Lawrence and Maclise. Details. From the
original working drawing dated October 1901.

82 (overleaf, left)
Maclise House. View of the courtyard from Herrick Street.
83 (overleaf, right)
Lawrence House. A courtyard entrance.

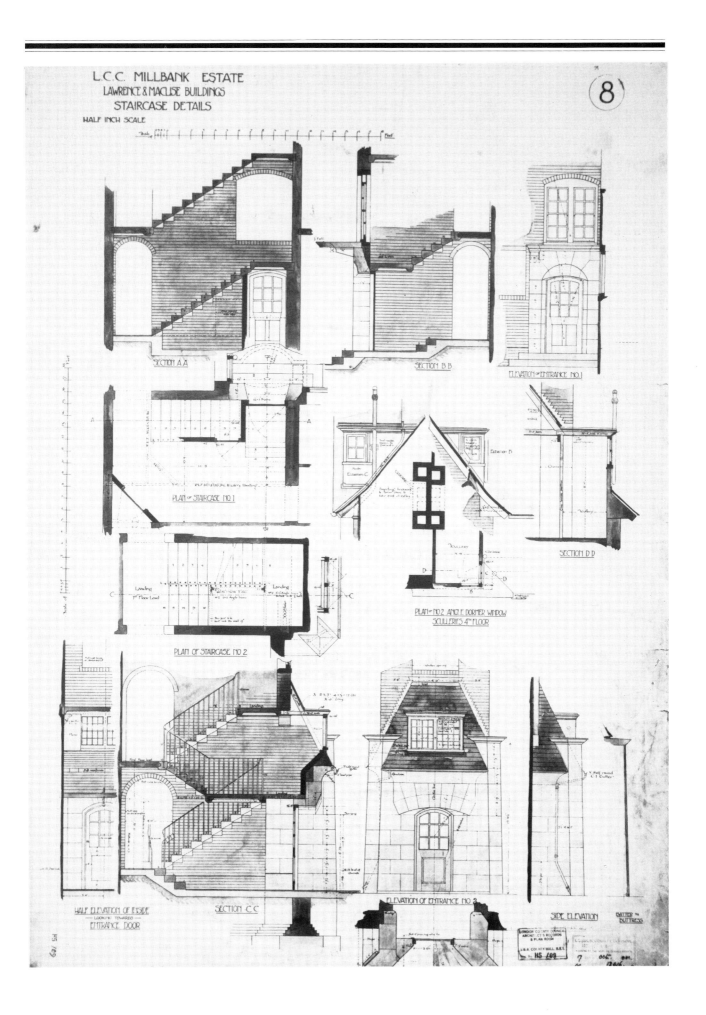

L.C.C. MILLBANK ESTATE
LAWRENCE & MACLISE BUILDINGS
STAIRCASE DETAILS
HALF INCH SCALE

SECTION A A

SECTION B B

ELEVATION OF ENTRANCE NO. 1

PLAN OF STAIRCASE NO 1

PLAN OF STAIRCASE NO 2

PLAN OF NO 2 ANGLE DORMER WINDOW
SCULLERIES 4TH FLOOR

SECTION D D

HALF ELEVATION OF INSIDE
ENTRANCE DOOR

SECTION C C

ELEVATION OF ENTRANCE NO 2

SIDE ELEVATION

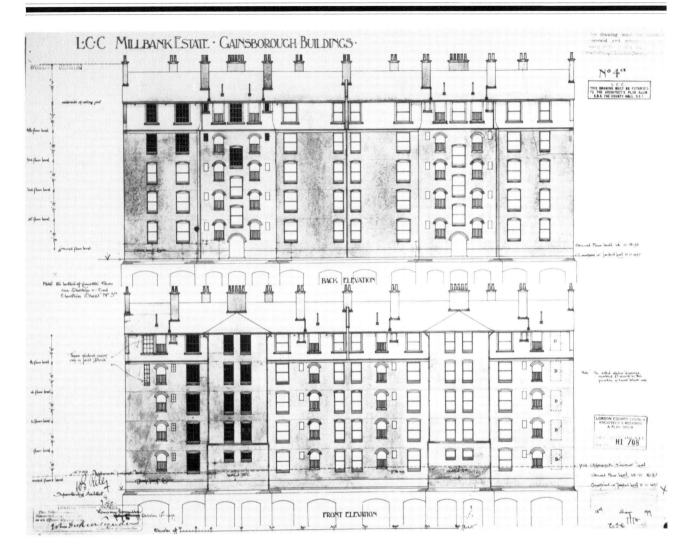

Millbank is unique among LCC flatted estates of the period in having been the object, *at the time of its erection*, of wholehearted critical acclaim. In 1900 the spring visit of the Architectural Association was held there, attracting 'a large attendance of members' – the peers, that is, in the closest sense, of the architects of the Housing branch. W Bonner Hopkins's record of the visit, published in the subsequent issue of *AA Notes*, deserves to be quoted at some length for it remains the most sensitive tribute ever made to the visual qualities of the Estate.[76] 'The whole of the joinery', Hopkins noted first, 'is of the simplest description, the sash bars of the windows being of a strong unmoulded square section . . . the verges (of the roofs) overhang some inches, and are formed in coke breeze concrete. This is considerably tilted, which both serves the practical purpose of throwing the wet away from the edges of the gables, and gives a pleasant effect. The underside of the verges is sloped up from the wall face to the edge of the tiles, and plastered and whitewashed, forming a pleasing finish, both in colour and form. The chimney shafts are capped with a moulded corona brick and look very well indeed'. His most fervent admiration was reserved for Hogarth House itself: 'Of the buildings at present only one or two are finished to the top, with the exception of the block built by the County Council's own Works Department, which was been some time completed. This building is on the axis of the layout of the estate, and faces the back of the National Gallery of British Art. It is an extremely good example of a building which owes its interest (and that of no mean quality) entirely to its good proportions and charming disposition of masses, together with the well harmonised colours of the materials. The central gable is very well designed. The walls are of red brick, with bands of blue-grey bricks at intervals in the upper parts. The water closet excrescences are additions to the excellence of the design instead of eyesores as they too frequently seem; some of them are formed into octagonal turrets which have quite a collegiate appearance, and others, having their side walls slightly sloped into the main wall of the building, seem to grow out of the latter and to cling to it in a way that makes them part of the whole, rather than ugly and unwelcome necessities. Two small whitewashed gables add a note of colour contrast which has a valuable effect, and the tall grey-green slated roofs make a finish very satisfactory in form and colour. The whole design reflects the greatest credit on those gentlemen in the Architect's Department of the London County Council who are responsible for it. The interior of the building was

visited, an empty flat being inspected. The corridors and staircases are finished in pressed red bricks built fair faced, and they are very satisfactory in appearance. The wood-work, joiners' ironmongery and the few mouldings are all refined in design and carefully executed. Ornament in the usual acceptation of the term is entirely absent; the building owing to this and its complete freedom from the least vulgarity of detail, together with its pleasing proportions, mass, line and colour, being a salve for the sore eyes of the architects of today'.

In the echoing opinion of the *Architectural Review*'s critic writing in 1905, 'There is a reasonableness and picturesqueness of disposition as well as a certain simple refinement of treatment about these dwellings which is very pleasant. . . .'.[77] The Estate was completed in August 1902, and has recently been modernised internally. Those qualities singled out for special praise by Hopkins and the *Review* have ensured that its elegance remains undiminished today, a stirring memorial, not only to the Housing branch, but to Victorian social conscience and to the com-mitted endeavour of local government to improve the quality of Londoners' lives.

84 (*facing page*)
Gainsborough House. Elevations. From the original working drawing dated May 1899.
85 (*above*)
Gainsborough House, Erasmus Street front.

·3·

·THE·BRANCH· ·UNDER·NEW· ·LEADERSHIP·

In 1899 Thomas Blashill retired from the Council's service and the Housing branch began a new chapter in its history. Change was in the air, not simply because of the arrival of a new Architect but because in 1898 the concept of the suburban *cottage* estate had entered the Council's housing policy and was waiting to be explored. Blashill's successor William Edward Riley came to County Hall from the Admiralty where he had been employed since 1877 and had risen to the position of Assistant Director of Architectural and Engineering Works.[78] Riley's architectural reputation has benefited, frequently at Blashill's expense, from widespread misunderstanding of the role of an official architect. The character of the Housing branch and the quality of LCC architecture had been firmly established by staff engaged long before Riley came to County Hall. Like Blashill, he was essentially an administrator. To credit him, as H L Curtis did in 1937, with having 'adopted the architectural language of [Norman] Shaw' is virtually meaningless, however reasonable the succeeding claim that he took responsibility for works which were 'wholly admirable in their frank expression of the function of the building and the method of its construction'.[79] His friend Frederick Hiorns who was himself appointed Architect to the Council in 1939, gave a more balanced view when he wrote, shortly after Riley's death, that '. . . his powers of organisation placed him in the forefront of administrators' and that, as to the LCC's great building programme, 'it would be no injustice to him to suggest that the credit it brought should be shared by the men he gathered round him'.[80] Nevertheless, Riley's most important contribution to the Housing branch before the war was the reorganisation of existing staff: it is doubtful whether any of the new recruits he 'gathered round him' matched Blashill's men of the '90s in calibre as designers.

In 1900 Owen Fleming and Charles Winmill were transferred to the Fire Brigade branch where they made an immediate and profound impact upon the design of fire stations, bringing them, as they had brought housing, into the mainstream of the Arts and Crafts movement. Fleming was replaced at first by John Briggs from General section who had joined the Metropolitan Board of Works in 1886 at the age of twenty-seven.[81] In 1902 Briggs went on to become Chief Assistant Architect to the Council, leaving Rob Robertson as head of Housing. A few months later Reginald Minton Taylor also left to join the General section.

T G Charlton having resigned in 1898, the only senior members of the original group to remain in Housing were William Hynam and A M Philips. Neither of these, however, appears to have initialled drawings during Riley's administration: after the completion of Millbank a new group of men between five and ten years younger than the first began to make their mark upon the branch's house-style. How faithful they were to it, how they refined or weakened it, may be detected in the sequence of flatted schemes initiated by the Council between 1900 and 1910, and divided among them.

The evidence of the surviving initialled plans suggests that the three most active designers in the branch at this period were J R Stark, J G Stephenson and E H Parkes. All three were promoted within a few months of Riley's appointment from the rank of temporary assistant to permanent assistant, 1st class.

James Rogers Stark was born in 1870. In 1887 he was articled to John Bressey and from 1891 to 1895, while continuing to work as an assistant to Bressey and Walters, studied at the AA where he became a prize medallist. He joined the Housing branch in 1895 and retired in 1934. When Stark was recommended by Leonard Stokes, W E Riley and Halsey Ricardo in 1911 as a candidate for licentiate membership of the RIBA, he listed among his works up to that time, 'Holiday Home, Sandon, Essex; House, Grove Park, Wanstead; Memorial Home for Aged Women, King Edward Street, Spitalfields; Houses, Malford Grove, Wanstead', and, finally, for the LCC, 'Blocks of artizans' dwellings, cottages and lodging houses for men'.[82]

On the basis of initialled plans and the implications of his RIBA declaration form, three major works in central London may be attributed to Stark: the Webber Row Estate, Southwark and two lodging houses provided by the Council for single men, Carrington House, Deptford and Bruce House off Drury Lane, all still standing and in their original use. Webber Row was a slum area designated for clearance in 1899 but the rehousing scheme planned to accommodate 1,143 people was not begun until 1905. The five blocks lie, one behind the other, parallel to Waterloo Road, their end elevations fronting onto Webber Row. They are of closely similar design, Mawdley House, facing Waterloo Road, having shops on the ground floor (Plates 86–87). They are five storeys high with attics and are arranged on the balcony plan, access to the flats being from balconies running the whole length of the rear elevations. Once described as the Architect's Department's 'finest contribution to street design',[83] Webber Row reflects the ubiquitous influence of Boundary Street which had been well under way when Stark arrived in Housing. Yet the estate derives a special identity from the series of simple and idiosyncratic details which, it is tempting to assume, are the project architect's own inventions: huge curling wrought-iron eaves brackets and neat bands of brickwork laid in a pattern of recessed crosses (Plate 88), volutes flaring boldly from otherwise strictly rectilinear balcony railings (Plate 89), quaint scalloped beams over austere staircase entrances (Plate 90). The same intense and almost whimsical concern for detail emerges in the design of Bruce House, Kemble Street, Westminster, of 1904, the working drawings for which are now, like the building itself, in the care of Westminster City Council (Plates 91–95). A massive six storeys high and built at a cost of £47,105 to shelter 700 people, the structure might have had an aspect as forbidding as its internal amenities were austere. Above the ground floor long rows of regularly-spaced windows express the tiny units of the cubicles

ranged down the corridors of the E-shaped plan. And yet the façade contrives, nevertheless, to suggest refuge, warmth and dignity. The broad-arched entrance is hollowed out of the front like the mouth of a cave and to the right of it the windows of the smoking-room are set waist-high from the pavement, their great arches and beautifully proportioned glazing bars devised to give, from within, at once a generous view of the street and a sense of seclusion from the glances of passers-by. Beyond the entrance, to the left of the main block and extending through to the Kean Street front, lay the superintendent's living-quarters – justification, if any were needed, for the sweet informality and domestic scale that characterises this part of the elevation. The railings that enclose the basement area are evidence of a growing preoccupation with the design of iron-work. With their customary hatred of standardization LCC architects would produce new ideas for iron-work whenever it was required: the fine detailing here is unique to Bruce House, a last defiant assertion of its individuality.

'The provision of lodging houses', stated the LCC's housing handbook of 1913, 'has been a distinctive and interesting feature of the Council's policy with regard to the housing of the working classes'. Architecturally as well as socially the lodging houses project is of particular interest for it occasioned one of the Council's earliest attempts to divert design responsibility away from the Housing branch. The first LCC lodging house, completed in January 1893 in Parker Street, close by Bruce House, was designed by the firm of Gibson and Russell (Plate 96). Architects of no mean reputation in the field of public buildings, they worked in a mild Baroque style dependent, like their West Ham Technical Institute and Library of 1895, on the lavish use of sculpture and other decorative devices for its rich and impressive effect. In order to meet the stringent demands of the Council's budget on the Parker Street site, however, Gibson and Russell were forced to drastically reduce this kind of ornament – to reduce it, indeed, to one feature, the bracketed entrance hood that juts incongruously from the bleak façade, accentuating the poverty of the general design. Carrington House, Brookmill Road, Deptford of 1902, with its monumental curving façade and pavilioned roof, was the second LCC lodging house and the first to be entrusted to Stark and his colleagues (Plate 97). To compare its architectural qualities with those of Parker Street House is to appreciate, not only how exceptionally high the Housing branch's aesthetic standards were, but how skilled its architects had become in reconciling those standards with minimal financial resources. At Carrington House they excelled Gibson and Russell in achieving a slightly lower cost per unit of accommodation. At Carrington House – almost as if inviting comparison with Parker Street – a hooded portico of Portland stone provides the only purely decorative feature (Plate 98). Yet here it is no mere appendage but the climax of a vigorous and sophisticated design. Once more, the ideals of Lethaby come hauntingly

L.C.C. SOUTHWARK AREAS. WEBBER ROW SITE.
BLOCKS B.C.D.E.F.

SHEET Nº 63.
WORKING DRAWING Nº 16.

FRONT ELEVATION BLOCK F.

SCALE OF FEET.

88 (left)
Mawdley House. Detail of front elevation.
89 (bottom left)
Mawdley House. Detail of rear elevation.
90 (below)
Mawdley House. Entrance on rear elevation.

86 (facing page, top)
*Mawdley House, Webber Row Estate, Waterloo Road,
Southwark.*
87 (facing page, bottom)
*Mawdley House. Front elevation. From the original working
drawing dated October 1905.*

91 (top)
Bruce House, Kemble Street, Westminster. View from Drury Lane.
92 (above)
Bruce House. Entrance.
93 (left)
Bruce House. Detail of entrance arch.

94 (above)
Bruce House. Detail of Kemble Street front, superintendent's quarters.
95 (left)
Bruce House. Detail of railings.

to mind. Offering advice to church architects in 1889 he wrote, '. . . four square walls, with the foil of a dainty window, is all we want; petty architectural forms are added, and all fit expression is gone. Thicken the walls, heighten the parapets, save all you can of moulding and "carving", not worth a handful of field flowers any of it, and seek to have a piece of Fine Art by proportion and adjustment of parts alone, with just a point of high interest, it may be, in a little sculpture by a master's hand'.[84] Like the porches of Millbank, the great sculptural form of the entrance hood furnishes precisely that 'point of high interest' in a façade which achieves the status of art 'by proportion and adjustment of parts alone'.

The Housing architects' ever-increasing problem of maintaining freshness of approach and individuality of character in scheme after repetitive scheme was tackled after 1900 with widely varying results. Two of the most successful flatted estates begun during the first decade of the new century are the Caledonian, Islington (Plates 99–103) and Chadworth Buildings, Lever Street, Finsbury (Plates 104–105). Both may be attributed to John Greenwood Stephenson, the first on the evidence of drawings initialled by him and dated 1904, the second, completed in 1907, on stylistic grounds alone for the drawings have been lost since their transfer, with the care of the estate, to the Borough of Islington.

Born in 1872, Stephenson was a student at the South Kensington Schools and at the AA of which he became a member in 1890. In 1892-3 he worked in the office of Sir Arthur Blomfield, first as an improver and then as a draughtsman, and he joined the Housing branch in 1894. With Blomfield, Blashill and John Slater as sponsors, Stephenson was elected Associate of the RIBA in 1896 but his declaration form only confirms that he had been previously employed as a draughtsman in the Council's housing section. On the evidence of initialled drawings he was later engaged with James Stark and others on the designs for the pre-war cottage estate at Norbury. He is known to have been directly concerned, after the war, with the Roehampton and White Hart Lane cottage estates and to have been appointed resident officer on those at Downham and St Helier. He remained in Housing until his retirement in 1937.[85]

The blocks forming the principle quadrangle of the Caledonian Estate are built on the balcony plan, here used by Stephenson as the basis for a masterly exercise in Arts and Crafts design. The grid of horizontals and verticals established in the balconies and living-room bays is reinforced in the ground floor arcades and massive buttressed entrance blocks. Its severe geometry serves to heighten each contrast of solid with void and light with shade and to sharpen the effect of each modest flourish of decoration in iron- and brickwork. The estate's specially-designed garden gates and balcony railings play an important part in creating a sense of place and special identity. Like their counterparts at Rushworth and Boyfield Street, Bruce House and Webber Row and even the simplest flatted

blocks such as Mallory House, St John Street (Plate 106), they are among the finest examples of architectural ironwork to have been produced in London at this period.

Stephenson's two Islington estates enrich the LCC housestyle and remain faithful to its principals. The Bourne Estate in Holborn represents another, less appealing line of development for it exhibits the first signs of a gradual drift away from the group's radical ideals. Begun in 1901 and completed, with the addition of Union Buildings, in 1907, Bourne is now in the care of the Borough of Camden, as are also the working drawings that relate to it. Built to house some 3,900 people at high density, it is the only pre-war LCC flatted estate that approaches Boundary Street and Millbank in size. The main part of the site is defined by blocks fronting onto Portpool Lane, Leather Lane and Clerkenwell Road (Plates 107–108). These are linked by archways giving onto a central court where six similar blocks are ranged in parallel rows with narrow strips of garden between (Plates 109–110). The flats were planned, like those of the Caledonian Estate, on the then somewhat unpopular system of open balcony access but much was made of the care with which the system had been applied here. 'The internal blocks lie north and south', the Council's housing handbook explains, 'so that the maximum of sunlight is obtained for the living rooms, and each tenement has at least one room looking on to a garden. The plan is an improved balcony plan, arranged so that the living room and the bedroom windows have unobstructed light, but do not look onto the balconies'.[86] The disproportionately large amount of descriptive text and illustrations given to the Bourne Estate in LCC housing handbooks echoes the equally biased view expressed by W E Riley in 1909 when he addressed the RIBA on 'The Architectural Work of the London County Council'.[87] This was evidently a scheme of which the Council was particularly proud. It is also unique among flatted schemes completed before 1913 for the paraphernalia of Edwardian classicism adorning its façades. At a time when the Edwardian Grand Manner dominated civic design in England, there must have been many in County Hall who felt that pediments and pilasters and weighty cornices were a more fitting expression of the Council's magisterial role than the simple self-effacing architecture of Rushworth Street or Webber Row. It was inevitable, perhaps, that the Housing branch should respond sooner or later to such pressures: the initials of Ernest Hadden Parkes on the working drawings for the Bourne Estate imply that he was the first member of the group to do so.

96 (*facing page, top left*)
Parker Street House, Parker Street, Westminster. Designed by Gibson and Russell, 1892.
97 (*facing page, top right*)
Carrington House, Brookmill Road, Lewisham.
98 (*facing page, bottom*)
Carrington House. Detail of entrance.

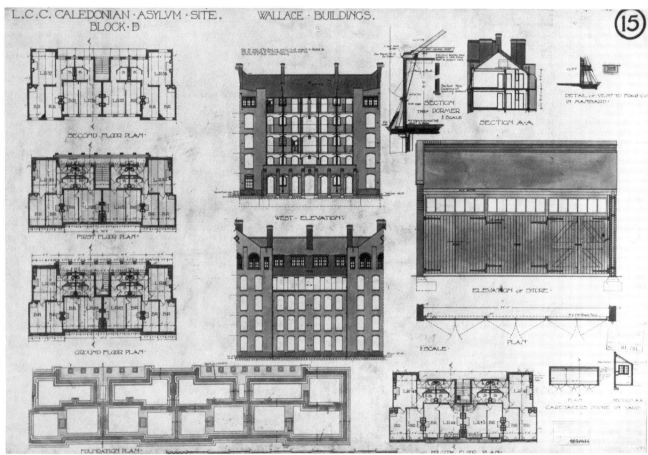

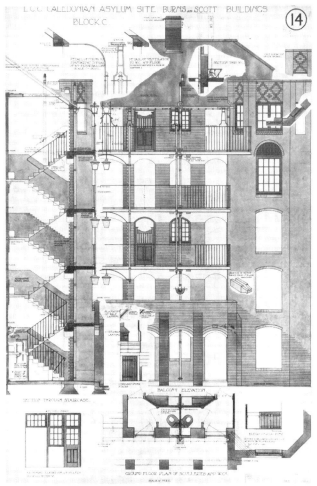

99 (*facing page, top*)
Caledonian Estate, Caledonian Road, Islington. View in quadrangle.
100 (*facing page, bottom*)
Wallace House, Caledonian Estate. Plans, elevations and sections. From the original working drawing dated September 1904.
101 (*above*)
Caledonian Estate. Quadrangle. Detail of arcading.
102 (*top*)
Caledonian Estate. Quadrangle. Detail of balconies.
103 (*right*)
Caledonian Estate. Quadrangle. Details of balcony elevation and section. From the original working drawing dated September 1904.

104 (*facing page, top left*)
Chadworth House, Lever Street, Islington. Entrance to quadrangle.
105 (*facing page, top right*)
Chadworth House. View in quadrangle.
106 (*facing page, bottom*)
Mallory House, 115–121 St John Street, Islington. Detail of shop front railings.

107 (*top left*)
Bourne Estate, Union Buildings, Camden. Angle block at junction of Leather Lane and Portpool Lane.
108 (*bottom left*)
Bourne Estate. Radcliff House, Clerkenwell Road, Camden.
109 (*top right*)
Bourne Estate. Entrance to courtyards through Radcliff House.

Parkes was born in 1866 and went to Tonbridge school. He attended the design classes of the AA from 1884 and served his articles with Sir Bannister Fletcher. He joined the staff of the LCC in January 1894. One of the first schemes that he supervised was an estate of three tenement blocks in Churchway, St Pancras, begun in 1900, and he was later much concerned with cottage estate development. He rose to the position of assistant architect in the Housing branch during the post-war period when the huge out-lying cottage estates at Dagenham, Bellingham and Becontree were in course of erection. He retired in 1931 and died twenty-two years later.[88] If the Bourne Estate is accepted as predominantly his work, Parkes must be credited with a major role in shaping the character of LCC flatted housing after the first world war. In these impassive elevations and ravine-like internal courts lie a foretaste of the arid neo–Georgian manner that was to engulf the identity of the branch during the 1920s.

Working alongside Stark, Stephenson and Parkes were several junior designers who seem to have been individually responsible for a series of small flatted estates, each comprising a single five-storeyed block. Notable among these are D'Arcy House, London Fields, of 1902 (Plate 111) and Lennox House, Wandsworth Road, of 1903, their drawings initialled by P F Binnie and J G N Clift respectively. The British Architect remarked with approval how, at D'Arcy House, 'the large mass of building is made to tell picturesquely by the raised pavilion roofs, and the placing of the chimneys'[89] and both blocks faithfully reproduce the pleasant domestic scale and air of informality which had been established at Boundary Street as the basis of the LCC house-style. Yet the variable quality of the smaller estates points to an increasing neglect, after 1900, of those architectural ideals for which the branch had fought during the 1890s. It is perhaps more than a coincidence that Durham Buildings, Wandsworth, of 1902, among the grimmest testimonies of that neglect, should have descended rapidly into squalor and itself become the worthy subject of a slum clearance scheme (Plate 112).

110 (*left*)
Bourne Estate. View of courtyard. From an LCC photograph.
111 (*overleaf, top*)
D'Arcy House, London Fields, Tower Hamlets.
112 (*overleaf, bottom*)
Durham Buildings, York Road, Wandsworth. (Demolished.) From an LCC photograph.

·4·

·THE·COTTAGE· ·ESTATES·

During its early years in the role of housing authority the LCC had been principally concerned with rehousing under Parts I and II of the 1890 Act: that, is with the provision of dwellings for people made homeless by slum clearance and road improvement schemes. Not until November 1898 did the Housing Committee resolve to take full advantage of the powers it possessed under Part III – to buy and build upon vacant land with the purpose of actually creating new – that is, additional – accommodation in the London area.[90] Behind the decision lay the Council's intent to embark upon a form of housing that was at once quite new and the centre, at that moment, of lively public interest.

The housing of working class people in urban communities of terraced cottages was of course not new at all but a tradition that embraced schemes as early as Saltaire near Bradford begun in 1851 and as close at hand in time and place as the low-rise suburban housing erected by the Artizans' Labourers' and General Dwellings Company at Battersea in 1872 and in west Kilburn in 1877 (Plate 113). The LCC itself had on several occasions erected cottages, albeit arranged in flats, as an alternative to block dwellings. The first people displaced by the Boundary Street clearance had been rehoused at nearby Goldsmith's Row in brick cottages designed, according to his daughter and the evidence of initialled drawings, by C C Winmill (Plate 114). In 1895 A M Philips had initialled plans for Hughes Fields cottages, destined to rehouse, in a long and monotonous row, 666 slum dwellers from Deptford (Plate 115). All these cottage schemes, from Saltaire to Hughes Fields, share, however, the same urban character; toeing a rigid building line, they deny the possibility of accident and natural growth that is inherent in the idea of the village, just as their flat repeating units reject the concept of separate identity and individuality. That the Housing branch had not invariably been willing to accept the limitations of the workers' cottage tradition is implied in the two schemes, both now demolished, for people moved to make way for the building of the Blackwall Tunnel. By adopting the simplest elements of the vernacular revival, Robert Robertson in his Westview, Armitage and Collerston Cottages, Blackwall Lane, of 1893 (Plates 116–117) and Philips in his Idenden Cottages, Tunnel Avenue, of 1895 (Plates 118–119) achieved a somewhat cosier and more rural quality. They tried, too, to introduce an element of informality and variety in their layout of these tiny 'estates', but made no attempt to abolish the back projection, that hated symbol of slum planning.

Meanwhile the romantic idea of removing people from teeming and dirty city centres to houses with gardens in a more or less self-sufficient rural environment was steadily gaining ground. Its first complete expression in London had been Bedford Park, Acton, an estate of red brick villas laid out by Norman Shaw in 1876. Yet Shaw's very middle-class suburb, however successful architecturally, is a far cry from the radical reforms envisaged by William Morris when he spoke of the need to 'turn this land from

113 (left)
Shaftesbury Estate, West Kilburn, Westminster. Designed by
William Austin, 1876.
114 (below)
Cottages at Goldsmith's Row, Tower Hamlets.
115 (bottom)
Cottages at Hughes Fields, Greenwich.

116 (facing page, top)
Cottages at Blackwall Lane, Greenwich. (Demolished.)
Elevation and section. From the original working drawing
dated March 1893.
117 (facing page, bottom)
Cottages at Blackwall Lane. Plans. From the original working
drawing dated March 1893.

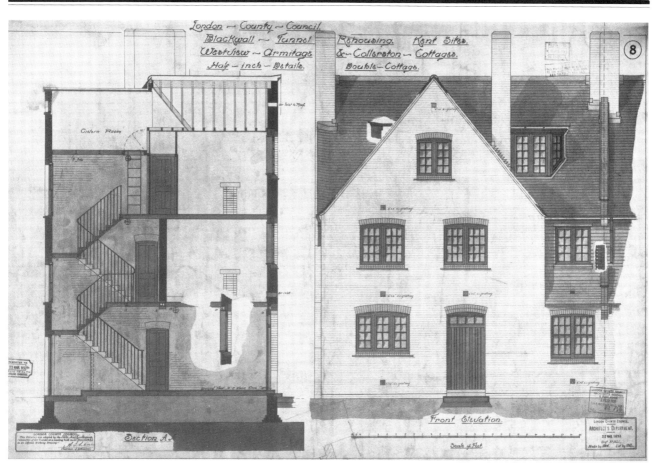

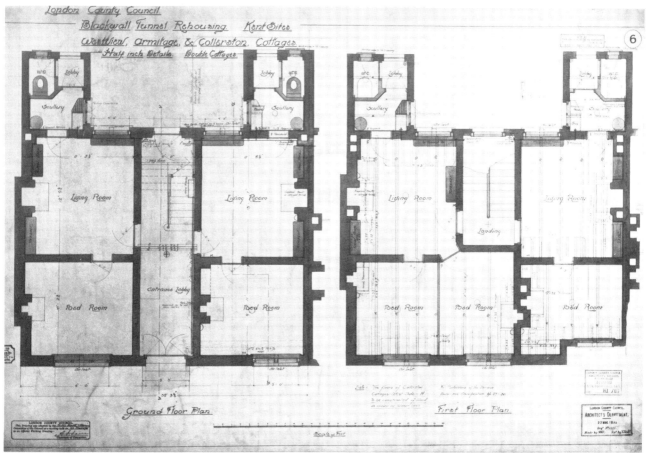

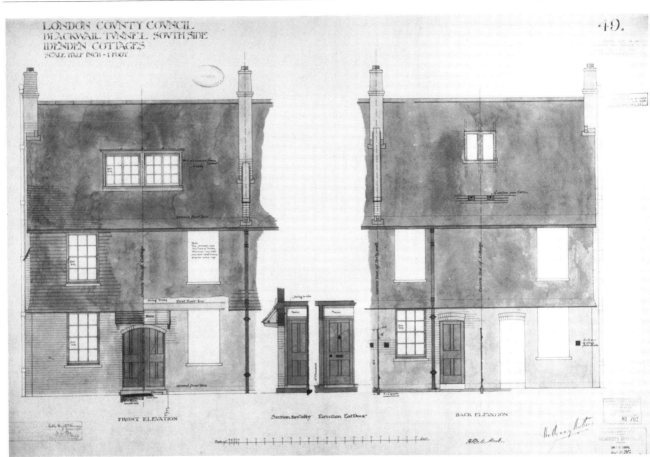

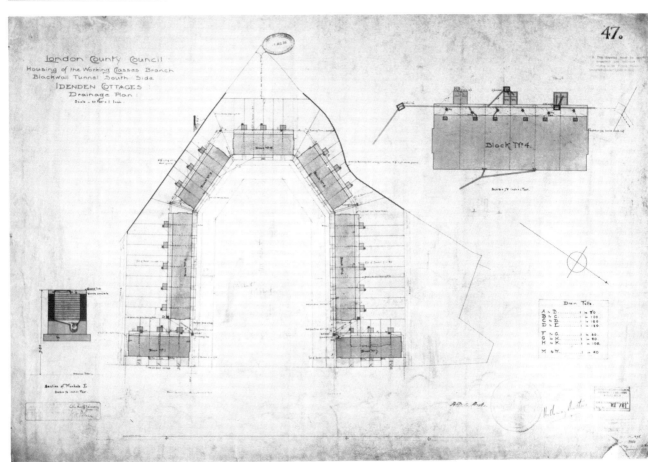

the grimy back yard of a workshop into a garden'.[91] The first steps towards adapting for the benefit of the poor the kind of idyll represented by Bedford Park were taken in the model villages for workers created in the 1890s – at Port Sunlight by the Lever brothers and at Bournville by the Cadburys. These heralded an extraordinary explosion of activity in housing and town-planning theory, practice and legislation. In 1898 Ebenezer Howard, a Parliamentary reporter with a consuming interest in land reform, launched the 'Garden City' movement with the publication of his book *Tomorrow: a Peaceful Path to Real Reform* (revised in 1902 under the new and now more familiar title *Garden Cities of Tomorrow*). The following year the Garden City (later Garden City and Town Planning) Association was formed to promote the ideas that Howard had put forward. In 1900 a new Housing Act enabled local councils intending to build housing under Part III of the 1890 Act to do so *outside* their own territory: thus providing them with the powers they needed to build garden suburbs.[92] In 1901 the architect-planners Barry Parker and Raymond Unwin who had formed a partnership in 1896 published their first book, *The Art of Building a Home*, and in November of the same year Unwin addressed the annual meeting of the Workmen's National Housing Council (formed in 1898) on 'The Housing of the Working Classes'. The lecture, it was reported, 'was well illustrated by . . . plans of the numerous efforts of municipalities and others to meet the want, which were used by the lecturer chiefly as examples of what to avoid. He compared the existing system of laying out artisans' dwellings in streets with the plan of arranging them in quadrangles advocated by him'. The commentator went on to remark that in his opinion Unwin's ideal schemes were 'more suitable for the country than the heart of London'. He had been interested to see on the screen several studies of cottages at Port Sunlight and Bournville and had noticed that 'several delegates from London municipal building committees were present and took part in the discussions'.[93] It is difficult to imagine that the LCC ignored this meeting or that the Housing branch itself was unrepresented there.

Parker and Unwin's Fabian Tract, *Cottage Plans and Commonsense*, was addressed specifically to 'public authorities engaged in Housing the People under the new Act of 1900' and appeared in 1902. Stating that in their opinion the best answer to the housing problem was to build attractive cottages conveniently placed for access to work and centres of interest and amusement, they suggested that, apart from considerations of health and economy, the most important factor in the development of a successful town suburb was that cottages should possess 'a simple dignity and beauty . . . which assuredly is necessary, not only to the proper growth of the gentler and finer instincts of men, but to the producing of that indefinable something which makes the difference between a mere shelter and a home'.[94] Their reputation as town-planners fast gathering momentum, the two men were engaged by Joseph Rowntree in 1902 to lay out and prepare designs for the model village of New Earswick, York, which he had started in rivalry with Bournville and in response, too, to Howard's *Garden Cities of Tomorrow*. During the same year the Garden City Pioneer Company Ltd was founded, 'To promote and further the distribution of the industrial population upon the lines suggested in Mr. Ebenezer Howard's book . . . and to form a garden city, that is to say, a town or settlement for agricultural, industrial, commercial and residential purposes, or any of them, in accordance with Mr. Howard's scheme or any modification thereof'. In 1903 a site was found at Letchworth and the Company commissioned Parker and Unwin to prepare a plan for the first garden city.

Amidst such activity the architects and planners of the LCC's Housing branch launched the first cottage suburb housing programme ever undertaken by a public authority. The relationship of their work to the Garden City Movement as a whole is difficult to define. The ideas they undoubtedly shared with its promoters would have been constantly tempered by tight financial controls and other expediencies. The density of cottages to the acre at Port Sunlight was 8: on LCC estates it varied between 21 and 32. Yet, steering a middle course between their own well-tried and practical vernacular style and the picturesque conceits of the model villages, listening to the reforms preached by Ebenezer Howard and Raymond Unwin, and keeping a watchful eye on comparable work then being produced by revered contemporaries such as Thackeray Turner (Plate 120), they created a modified form of garden city that introduced thousands of working class people to a new style of life and is no less remarkable a contribution to the movement for having gone largely unrecognised within it. When Hermann Muthesius wrote *Das Englische Haus* he was apparently unaware that the Council was already far advanced with its first cottage estate on a site at Tooting. He had heard, however, of the scheme to build a similar estate at Tottenham, begun in 1904, the year of his book's publication, and welcomed it enthusiastically as part of the garden city movement, evidence of a growing awareness that the building of tall blocks of flats in city centres did not strike at the roots of the working class housing problem.[39]

The Totterdown Fields Estate of approximately 39 acres at Tooting, conveniently close to a railway station and to the Council's own tramways, became LCC property in January 1900 for the sum of £44,238. It was laid out for development on a grid system of parallel streets (Plate 121): Lessingham Avenue, the principal and central thoroughfare which runs in a gradual curve from

118 (*facing page, top*)
Idenden Cottages, Tunnel Avenue, Greenwich. Elevations.
From the original working drawing dated May 1895.

119 (*facing page, bottom*)
Idenden Cottages, Tunnel Avenue. Drainage plan. From the original working drawing dated May 1895.

Upper Tooting Road on the north-west to Church Lane on the south-east, is 45 feet wide and lined with trees, as also are two of the streets that cross it at right angles, Blakenham Road and Franciscan Road. The remaining subsidiary streets are 40 feet wide. The cottages that flank them are all two storeys high and built of bricks, varying in colour from a warm red to yellow and a bluish-grey. Other simple variations of colour and texture are achieved with the introduction here and there of a cement render on the gables and upper storeys, sometimes left smooth in its natural sandy colour, sometimes painted white or given a rough-textured grey finish with pebble dash (Plates 122–127). Occasionally a glazed brick trim is used to enliven a doorway or a yellow stock brick elevation is dressed with red bricks. (The appearance of some of the terraces has been spoilt, recently, by the application of red paint to the ground storey brickwork). Windows are small-paned, mainly with sash frames painted white, though the external woodwork of many cottages was originally red and green, according to a contemporary observer (see page 97). The line of the street frontage is broken into short terrace lengths of up to twenty units set between twelve and twenty feet apart and lying back from the roads by distances varying from five to fifteen feet.

All the cottages – except for the few designed as flats – were provided with miniature garden plots at front and back and many had bathrooms. Their tiny frontages – as little as twelve feet wide in the three-bedroomed type and

calling for the most ingenious feats of compression in planning – had been forced upon the architects by Council policy. The first governing factor in the planning of Totterdown, explains the housing handbook, was 'economy of land and of road construction', to be achieved, it was decided, 'by limiting the frontage of plots where possible to narrow widths'.[95] Yet the accompanying resolve, to avoid wherever possible the back projections to which narrow frontages habitually gave rise, was in perfect accordance with the spirit of town-planning reform. Simultaneously, in *Cottage Plans and Common Sense*, Parker and Unwin were demanding the complete abolition of 'backs, and backyards, back alleys and other such abominations, which have been too long screened by the insidious excuse of that wretched prefix back'. Similarly, the guidance they offered on the design of working class cottages echoed principles that the Housing branch had applied to flatted estates for nearly a decade and was about to extend to the architecture of Totterdown. Variety and attention to detail, the town planners advised, were just as important as healthy planning: 'an elegant mould or shaping costs no more than a vulgar one, and a well-proportioned door or mantle is as easily made as one ill-proportioned. That nothing can be spent on the ornamentation of artisans' cottages is no excuse whatever for their being ugly. Plain and simple they must be, but a plain and simple building well designed may be very far from ugly'.

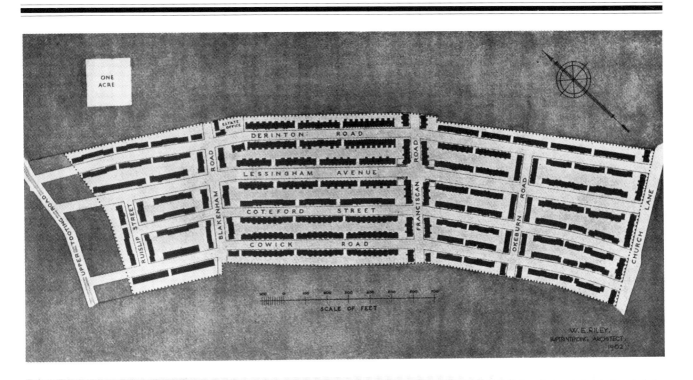

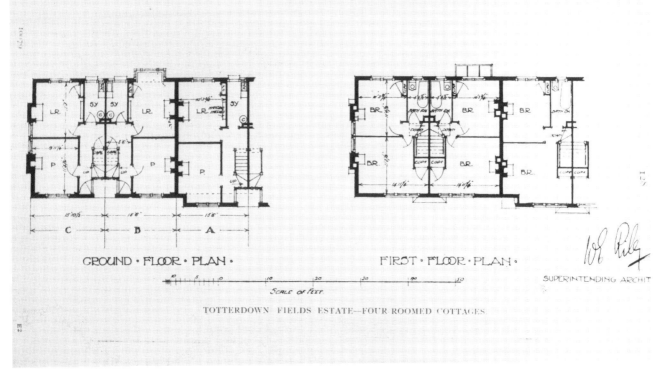

TOTTERDOWN FIELDS ESTATE—FOUR-ROOMED COTTAGES

Among Totterdown's most appealing qualities is the resource with which routine standardization has been avoided and the limitations its avenues share with the traditional working-class by-law street have been camouflaged or overcome. The division of terraces into short lengths, each carefully modelled and defined by projecting central or end bays, the introduction of gables to interrupt the line of roofs or sweep comfortably low over ground floor windows, are devices employed to counteract the effects of the grid-plan and its characteristic by-product, the seemingly endless vista of repeating units. Consciously

120 (*facing page*)
The Court, Buryfields, Guildford, Surrey. Designed by Thackeray Turner, c 1901.

121 (*top*)
Totterdown Fields Estate, Tooting, Wandsworth. Plan. From Housing of the Working Classes in London, *LCC, 1913, p 71.*

122 (*above*)
Totterdown Fields Estate. Plans of four-roomed cottages. From Housing of the Working Classes in London, *LCC, 1913, p 128.*

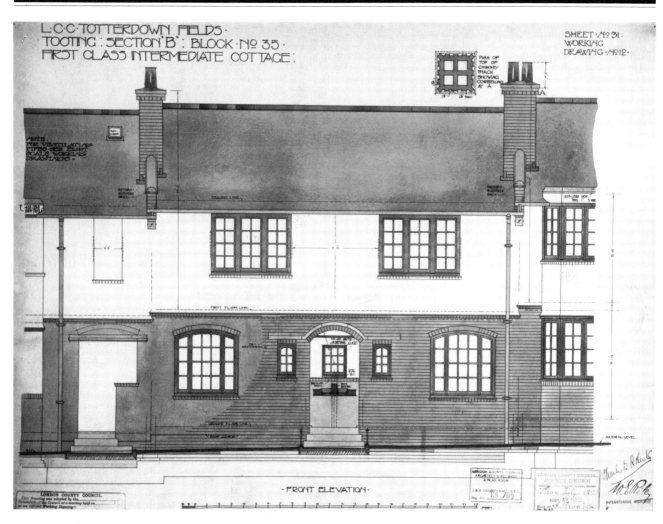

123 (*top*)
Totterdown Fields Estate. Elevation of a first class cottage. From the original working drawing dated July 1903.
124 (*left*)
Totterdown Fields Estate. Cottages in Blakenham Road.
125 (*above*)
Totterdown Fields Estate. Gabled cottages in Coteford Street.

126 (*above*)
Totterdown Fields Estate. Gabled cottages in Coteford Street.
127 (*left*)
Totterdown Fields Estate. Gabled cottages in Derinton Road.

128 (*overleaf, left*)
Totterdown Fields Estate. Paired entrances in Blakenham Road.
129 (*overleaf, right*)
Totterdown Fields Estate. Paired entrances in Derinton Road.

130 (*top*)
*House in Hampshire designed by Ernest Newton, illustrated in
his* Book of Country Houses, *1903, plate 44.*

131 (*above*)
*Mead Cottage, Buryfields, Guildford, Surrey. Designed by
Thackeray Turner, 1895.*

132 (*right*)
Totterdown Fields Estate. Cottages in Coteford Street.

or not, in their concern for the preservation of trees already on site and for establishing a varied but coherent architectural identity for their simple cottages, the Housing architects were responding to William Morris's call for urban renewal, for something better than the 'mere stretch of houses, the vast mass of shabbiness and uneventfulness (that) sits upon one like a nightmare'.[96] Bay windows too are used as a weapon against 'uneventfulness' and as a means of enlivening the view from tiny front rooms, just as *Cottage Plans and Common Sense* recommended. Windows facing the street, wrote Unwin, 'are much less depressing if slightly bayed to invite a peep up and down as well as across; a projection of a few inches in the centre, with some advantage of the thickness of the wall to set back the side, will suffice to add very much to the outlook'. It is in the gables and entrances of Totterdown that the richest display of invention is to be found. An astonishing variety of colours and ornamental forms is conjured from a range of materials and mouldings so basic that, while each cottage or group is thus distinguished from its neighbour, the coherence of the estate remains undisturbed. The pairing of entrances to read as a single architectural entity – charmingly complemented by the jasmine round a double porch in Blakenham Road (Plate 128) – not only helped to reduce the mean effect of successive small and close-set units but gave new scope for ingenuity in design (Plate 129). The cottage porches of Totterdown are delicate symbols of the Housing branch's resolve to bring the working class cottage within the same architectural context as the country house of the private patron: to establish the right of Council tenants to that flattering sense of identity and pride in uniqueness which the privileged expected to derive from their architectural environment. The social status of Ernest Newton's clients (Plate 130) or even of those who lived in Thackeray Turner's small cottage at Guildford (Plate 131) would have been far removed from that of the residents of Totterdown, yet the standards governing the design of their houses are as far as economically possible the same. 'Every part must be minutely schemed', wrote Ernest Newton in 1890, describing the ideal house, 'nothing should be cramped or mean looking, the whole house should be conceived broadly and simply, and with an air of *repose*, the stamp of home.'[97] Raymond Unwin now called, on behalf of the artisan, for 'a simple dignity and beauty' of architecture. The tiny cottages that serve as units in the larger design of the terraces at Tooting (Plate 132) demonstrate that the aims of Newton and Unwin were interchangeable and classless in their implications.

The first block of cottages was completed by the end of 1903 and the last by the summer of 1911. 1,229 houses and four shops were built in all, at a density of 31.81 to the acre. Their design and that of the three out-county estates which followed seems to have been very much a shared responsibility. However, the initials that appear most frequently on drawings for Totterdown are those of E Stone Collins. Born in 1874, Collins was trained in the office of E W Mountford. He entered the Architect's Department in April 1899 so that Totterdown must have been his first important project. Probably as a result of his work on it, he was promoted in July 1901 to the rank of 2nd class assistant and again in June 1903 to the lower division of the first class at a salary of £200 a year. In April 1908 he resigned and entered private practice. When Ralph Knott won the competition for the new County Hall, Collins was taken into partnership with him and in 1929 after Knott's early death he was selected to supervise the completion of the building. He died in 1942.[98] That Collins played a more than minor part in the conception of the Totterdown estate is confirmed by the fact that on the occasion of the Architectural Association's visit to Tooting in the spring of 1903, he was among the small group of architects, led by W E Riley, who conducted the party over the estate. The only other Housing branch officers in attendance were Hynam and, more significantly, Rob Robertson and A M Philips, both of whom laid claim to an important role in the estate's development. The occasion was a success and the LCC's work much admired. Louis Ambler who wrote an account of the visit in *AA Notes* appreciated the financial difficulties under which the architects had worked, pointing to the far lower densities achieved at Bournville and Port Sunlight. 'There is, however,' he remarked, 'no sense of overcrowding on the Council's estate, a result due to the skilful planning of the cottages and the clever laying out of the sites and roads, and great credit is due to the contrivers that hardly a tree will be destroyed, there being several good ones on the estate, and a fine row of elms, which an adjoining owner has agreed to leave standing, just beyond the boundary'. He went on to comment on the type plans, cost and size of rooms, comparing that of a living room in a 1st class cottage, 150 square feet, with that in a 4th class cottage flat, 130 square feet, and noting that the smallest area of all was the kitchen of a 4th class cottage, only 60 square feet. His sympathetic description of the estate is strongly reminiscent of Hopkins's account of Millbank, prompted, as on this occasion, by an AA visit (see page 68). 'The cottages,' wrote Ambler, 'are arranged in terraces and considerable variety has been given to their outlines and grouping. Economy being the great factor in the scheme, it is a matter for congratulation that the architectural character of the design is pleasing and varied, and though necessarily simple, in no way commonplace, but in strong contrast to the usual type of building erected for the working classes.

'The materials generally are London stock bricks of various specially selected tones, with salt-glazed bricks round the doorways, and red brick window arches, the upper parts of the walls being faced with rough-cast, some smooth and some "pebble-dashed". The eaves are finished square, with lath and plaster soffits, and the roofs are covered with Delabole slates. The external woodwork, etc, of some of the blocks is painted bright green and of others red. This adds to the cheerful appearance.

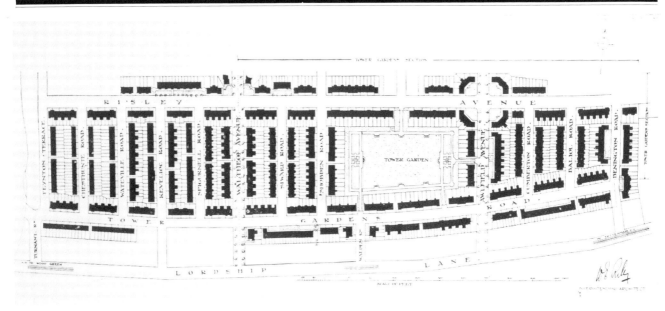

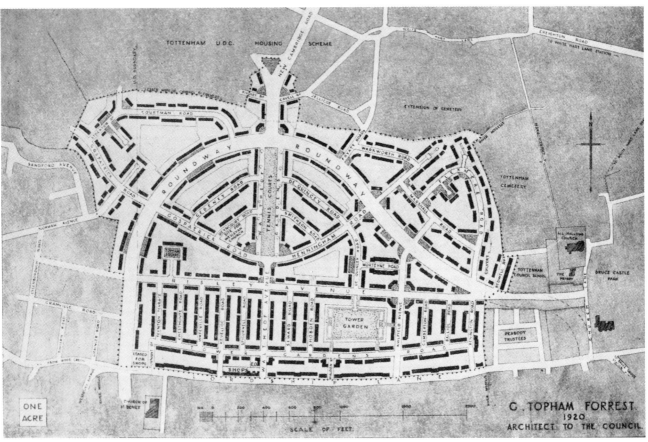

133 (top)
White Hart Lane Estate, Haringey, 1904–1914. From
Housing of the Working Classes in London, *LCC, 1913,*
p 75.
134 (above)
White Hart Lane Estate, showing post-war development.
From London Housing, *LCC, 1937, p 133.*

135 (facing page, top)
White Hart Lane Estate. Cottages in Chesthunte Road.
136 (facing page, bottom)
White Hart Lane Estate. Cottages in Chesthunte Road.
Front elevation. From the original working drawing dated
July 1903.

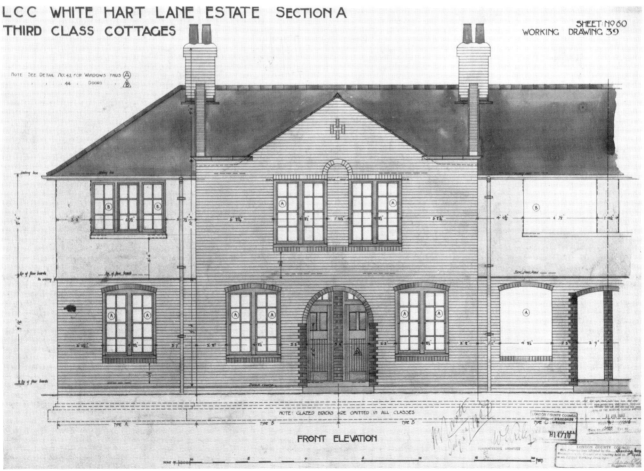

LCC WHITE HART LANE ESTATE SECTION A
THIRD CLASS COTTAGES

SHEET No 60
WORKING DRAWING 39

FRONT ELEVATION

'. . . The most noticeable feature in the planning is the entire absence of the back projection, a very great gain both in appearance and construction. The cottages look almost as well at the back as they do at the front, and the sun and air have full play all round. The closets are so planned that they are entered from an external lobby sunk in the back face of the buildings. Each cottage will have its own bit of front and back garden, except the 4th class [cottage flats] where the open yard at the back is common to four tenements. Internally the finishings are of the plainest description, mouldings being for the most part eschewed. The fireplaces of plain fire-bricks, with iron movable fronts and bottom grates, are very neat and economical and the portable ranges and coppers are substantial. All the rooms are well lighted and cheerful, and the outlook from each is pleasant. . . .'[99] Apart from Muthesius's brief comment in 1904 this seems to have been the only critical assessment of LCC cottage housing to appear in print before 1914. Little more than factual reporting accompanied the Housing architects' remarkable effort, in the three cottage estates which followed Totterdown, to improve upon their own prototype and to comply, as far as possible, with the highest ideals of the garden city movement.

The second piece of land acquired by the Council for cottage development was a large estate of 177 acres near White Hart Lane in Tottenham. Building began in 1904 on the west side of the southern section, between Lordship Lane and Risley Avenue, and by 1912 had reached the eastern boundary in Benington Road (Plate 133). The whole of the area to the north of Risley Avenue was laid out and developed after the war (Plate 134). The cottages in Chesthunte Road, like all those designed in 1903 for the western boundary, are closely similar in external treatment to the Totterdown Estate type (Plates 135–136). But with progress eastwards, new qualities began to emerge both in the articulation of façades and in terrace lay-out. The detailing of porches is richer and more decisive, the character of each group of cottages more distinct (Plates 137–139). There is an increasingly committed use of features recommended by Parker and Unwin: individual bay windows and two-storeyed canted bays give depth and modelling to the flat street frontage and projecting end bays hint at the formation of their beloved cottage 'quadrangles' (Plate 140). Slowly, almost stealthily, with each attempt at a bolder articulation of façade and terrace, the Housing branch moved closer to the ideal set forth in *Cottage Plans and Common Sense*: 'If, instead of being wasted in stuffy yards and dirty back streets, the space which is available for a number of houses were kept together, it would make quite a respectable square or garden. The cottages could then be grouped round such

137 (*left*)
White Hart Lane Estate. Cottages in Siward Road. From an LCC photograph.

open spaces, forming quadrangles opening one into the other, with wide streets at intervals. . . . There is something at once homely and dignified about a quadrangle which gives it a charm even when the buildings are quite simple and unadorned. There is a sense of unity, of a complete whole, which lifts it out of the commonplace in a manner that nothing can accomplish for a mere street of cottages. Each square could have some individuality of treatment, the entrances could be utilized to produce some little central feature, and the effect of thus grouping small cottages to produce collectively a larger unit in the street, of a scale capable of assuming some dignity, would be such an improvement as will not readily be realized by any who have not seen what a few simple college quads may do for an otherwise commonplace street . . .' (Plate 141).

The dream of adopting a more open, village-like plan at Tottenham became a reality when, in 1907, it was decided that the sum of £10,000 – donated by Lord Swaythling to aid the Council's housing programme – should be put towards the development of the southern section of the estate. The need for economy of land-use no longer so great, the streets on the western side were laid out round a miniature village green, the Tower Garden, turfed for tennis and bowls and surrounded by raised terraces and flower gardens. Individual house plots could be larger and terraces could be set further back from the road to form, with their returned end bays or with flanking terraces bordering on the road, shallow grassed enclosures or quadrangles (Plates 142–143). Among the most ambitious features of the Tower Garden area is the planning of the junction of Awlfield and Risley Avenues where cottages are arranged in four short curved angle blocks to overlook the crossroads, like large detached houses standing in their own grounds (Plates 144–145).

The average number of cottages to the acre on the southern section was 25.05, considerably less than the 31.81 density of Totterdown. However, a typical four-roomed cottage on the earlier estate cost £240. 14s to build, while its equivalent at White Hart Lane cost only £225 (Plates 122, 146). Questioned about this discrepancy at the RIBA in 1909, W E Riley remarked only, with a note of exasperation, that local Fletton bricks were being used for the Tottenham cottages while Kentish bricks had had to be brought long distances to the Tooting site and had therefore been more expensive. Weary of defending his Department against constant imputations of extravagance, he added brusquely that Council cottages were 'brick boxes with very little else'. If the brickwork could be done cheaply, the whole question of cost was solved. His RIBA paper reveals that Riley, like Blashill, had developed a vigorous cynicism in the face of the public's unyieldingly negative approach to the Council's housing programme. The failure of even the most informed and impartial critics to acknowledge the pioneering achievements of his Housing staff must, indeed, have been a bitter disappointment. 'Perhaps,' he reflected, 'there is no other professional man in the world who experiences more

criticism of his work than an architect, whether in private practice or in public service, and domestic architecture perhaps offers the widest scope. At all events, the architect who builds cottages for the working man gets an amplitude of criticism'. To demonstrate that much adverse comment was neither fair nor related to architectural values Riley told of an estate he knew 'on which cottages were built according to the estimates, and precisely according to the scheme on which the finances were based . . . without incurring one penny of embarrassing extras on the original proposal. After the houses were ready for letting only a few tenants were obtained. The local Press criticised the houses in the most severe manner, and they were practically boycotted. Why would they not let? Because, it was stated, the rooms were too small for one man to stretch himself comfortably at full length. Doors and windows were too small to admit bedsteads, and the doors, moreover, had quite a peculiar appearance because the panels were not according to stock pattern. Pianos refused to enter openings of such narrowness. The windows had such small panes that they might have belonged to prison cells. How could anyone see out of such small windows, or how could light get in? Surely, said the Press, all these were bad errors on the architect's part? Possibly, but the sequel was very interesting. Rents were lowered: with the result that bedsteads, pianos, and furniture of extraordinary dimensions for such small families found an entrance without even chipping the paint off the arrises of the same narrow doorways which had previously stood in the way of the letting of the houses. Thus it (will) be seen that the rent of a tenement (bears) a distinct relation to the width of the door; the windows with the small panes really looked quite well, and the light in the rooms had become so dazzling as to necessitate the purchase of elaborate curtains to subdue it. . . .' And so, said Riley in conclusion, he remained undiscouraged and when the time came for him to drop into oblivion as an ex-official he hoped to do so without repining, as many better men had done before him.[100]

The examining officers' initials that appear most frequently on drawings for the pre-war section of White Hart Lane are those of E P Wheeler, Arthur Floyd and Ernest Parkes, all of whom, it may be assumed, were working under the general supervision of A M Philips. Edwin Paul Wheeler, born in 1874, was apprenticed to the firm of Seale and Hayes of Ludgate Hill in 1891 and attended design classes at the AA between 1892 and 1896. He worked as an assistant to C J Dawson for five years before joining the Housing branch in 1899. He was

138 (facing page, top left)
White Hart Lane Estate. Paired entrances in Siward Road.
139 (facing page, top right)
White Hart Lane Estate. Paired entrances in Tower Gardens Road.
140 (facing page, bottom)
White Hart Lane Estate. Cottages in Waltheof Avenue.

141   (left)
'A quadrangle'. Reproduced from Cottage plans and Common Sense in The Legacy of Raymond Unwin, ed Walter L Creese, 1967, fig 10.
142   (centre left)
White Hart Lane Estate. Cottages in Risley Avenue.
143   (centre right)
White Hart Lane Estate. Cottages in Tower Gardens Road.
144   (bottom left)
White Hart Lane Estate. 180–186 Risley Avenue; angle block at the junction of Risley Avenue and Awlfield Avenue.
145   (bottom right)
White Hart Lane Estate. Rear elevation of 180–186 Risley Avenue.

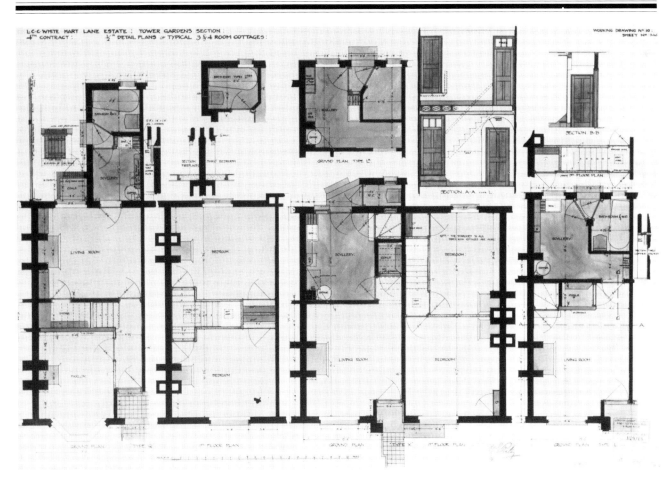

transferred, with J R Stark, to the Schools division in 1911 and in 1935 was appointed Architect to the Council. He died in 1944.[101] Floyd entered the Council's service in 1901 at the age of twenty-nine and by 1909 had risen in the Housing branch to the position of 1st class assistant. He retired in 1933.[41]

The Housing Act empowering local councils to erect working class dwellings on land lying outside their own district was passed in August 1900. The first area to be acquired by the LCC under the new Act was the Norbury Estate of some thirty acres near Croydon in Surrey, purchased for £18,000 in 1901. The earliest working drawings for cottages at Norbury are dated 1905 and development, which began at the eastern end of the estate near the main London Road progressed slowly across the rising ground towards Norton Gardens, the architectural as well as the geographical climax of the scheme. Designs for this last pre-war section date from 1909 and the remaining area, to the west of Norton Gardens, was completed after the war (Plate 147). The hillside site was a new challenge for the Housing branch and held interesting possibilities. Much use was made of the rise and fall of the land to enhance the sense of modelling and picturesque grouping in what remained, like Totterdown and White Hart Lane, essentially a grid lay-out of streets with a similar density of 29 cottages to the acre. The stepped and scrambled effect of the cottages in Norton Gardens and its sloping approach roads shows how far the branch had now

progressed from the flat and inflexible monotony of the standardized terrace (Plates 148–149). A new cluster of ideas for the decorative treatment of paired entrances was evolved for Norbury, ideas more reticent, perhaps, than their counterparts at Tooting and Tottenham, and suggesting that the branch was now concerned not so much with variety of detail as with contrasting general views and varied cottage groups (Plates 150–151). These later pre-war terraces contain, moreover, the first clear indications of the Housing architects' interest in that most celebrated of all contributions to the garden city movement, Hampstead Garden Suburb. Founded in 1906, the Suburb was widely publicized long before completion and many progressive architects, including Baillie Scott, Harrison Townsend and Edgar Wood, were to collaborate with Parker and Unwin and Edwin Lutyens in the design of its buildings. The low walls, brick paving and stepped approaches which contribute so much to the distinctive rural quality of the Norton Gardens area echo the features introduced by Baillie Scott – for precisely the same purpose – into his design for a quadrangle at the Suburb, never executed but published in 1908[102] (Plate 152). His idea

146 (above)
White Hart Lane Estate. Plans for typical 3 and 4 room cottages on the Tower Gardens section. From the original working drawing dated May 1909.

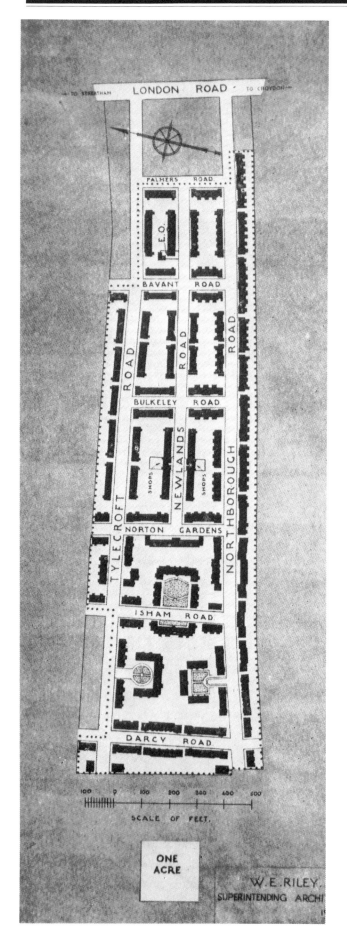

LONDON ROAD

PALMERS ROAD.

F.O.

BAVANT ROAD

ROAD

ROAD

ROAD

BULKELEY ROAD

NEWLANDS

SHOPS

SHOPS

NORTHBOROUGH

TYLECROFT

NORTON GARDENS

ISHAM ROAD

DARCY ROAD

SCALE OF FEET.

ONE
ACRE

W. E. RILEY,
SUPERINTENDING ARCH

was to be explored more fully and with remarkable success in the hillside quadrangle on Isham Road, erected, after the war, to the west of Norton Gardens (Plates 153–154).

Three architects appear to have been principally responsible for the Norbury Estate: J R Stark whose work for the Council at Webber Row and on the Carrington and Bruce lodging houses had recently been completed, P F Binnie, and George Weald. Peter Frederick Binnie, supervising officer for D'Arcy House, Hackney (Plate 111), joined the Housing branch in 1897 at the age of twenty-four, having worked previously in the offices of Theophilus Allen and Frank Bagallay and spent a short period as an assistant in the firm of Smith and Brewer, architects of the renowned Mary Ward Settlement in Bloomsbury. He rose rapidly within the Housing branch after 1901 and was promoted to the position of assistant architect in 1931. He retired six years later.[103] George Weald was born in 1874 and spent six years from 1890 as apprentice and assistant in the office of Norman Shaw. He attended the Royal Academy Schools from 1892 to 1897 and after 1896 worked with R W Schultz and F W Troup, entering the Housing branch in 1899. Weald was moved from Housing to Escape section in 1906 and from there to General section where he was concerned, in 1913, with the designs for Hammersmith Trade School for Girls, one of the most interesting products of the LCC Architect's Department at this period. On his RIBA Licentiate's declaration form Weald stated that he had been responsible for the design of the bandstand at Boundary Street (Plate 12) and that he had also executed 'various works for Gerald Horsley, E S Prior, W R Lethaby, Mervyn Macartney, Curtis Green and Christopher Turner'[104]. It is clear that Weald had a keen eye for architectural innovation: the rapid assimilation at Norbury of ideas generated by Hampstead Garden Suburb may owe much to his presence on the design team.

The culminating achievement of the Council's venture into garden suburb planning before the first world war is the Old Oak Estate, Hammersmith. The site, in some fifty-four acres lying immediately to the west of Wormwood Scrubs Prison, was bought for £29,858 in 1905 from the Ecclesiastical Commissioners. (Hence the naming of the new streets after Bishops of London.) The Great Western Railway Company then bought back eight acres of the Council's land for their new railway line which cuts diagonally across the estate from north-west to south-east. The pre-war development is contained within the triangle formed by the railway on the east, Old Oak Common Lane on the west and Du Cane Road on the south (Plate 155), and took place in two stages. Towards the end of 1909 the Architect was instructed to proceed with plans for roads and cottages bordering on and to the south of Erconwald Street. The earliest working drawings for cottages on this area are dated April 1911. The last drawings for the second contract, the area to the north of Erconwald Street, were made in August 1913. By the end of January 1914 304

147 (*facing page*)
Norbury Estate, Croydon. From London Housing, *LCC, 1937, p 131.*
148 (*above*)
Norbury Estate. Cottages in Norton Gardens.
149 (*left*)
Norbury Estate. Cottages in Northborough Road.

cottages and five shops had been erected, at a density of about 26 to the acre. The estate and its related drawings are now in the care of the Borough of Hammersmith and Fulham.

At Old Oak the influence of Hampstead Garden Suburb's pre-1911 development was completely assimilated and the Housing branch brought LCC cottage architecture to splendid maturity. The estate is separated from the Council's previous cottage suburbs not only by an interval of several years but by a piece of legislation which profoundly affected its lay-out and was largely a repercussion of Raymond Unwin's activities at Hampstead. In 1906 a private Act of Parliament was passed to enable Unwin to lay out the Suburb without the restrictions imposed by local building regulations. By-laws originally formulated to curb insanitary or hazardous planning had also had the effect of curbing inventiveness and flexibility. Buildings had to adhere to rigid building lines; the length and width of streets were strictly regulated and the continuous roofs of cottage terraces had to be monotonously divided into short lengths by parapets at their party walls. The Hampstead Garden Suburb Act of 1906, releasing Unwin from the need to follow many of these by-laws, opened the way for the introduction of closes and greens, squares and culs-de-sac on the estate plan. Colourful street views and vistas composed as carefully as painted landscapes were now real and exciting possibilities. Two years later in 1908, John Burns, President of the Local Government Board,

who had worked with Unwin on the 1906 Act, introduced his Housing and Town Planning Bill to Parliament. 'The object of the Bill,' he explained, 'is to provide a domestic condition for the people in which their physical health, their morals, their character and their whole social condition can be improved by what we hope to secure in this Bill. The Bill aims in broad outline at, and hopes to secure, the home healthy, the house beautiful, the town pleasant, the city dignified, and the suburb salubrious. It seeks, and hopes to secure, more homes, better houses, prettier streets, so that the character of a great people, in towns and cities and in villages, can be still further improved and strengthened by the conditions under which they live. . . . The Bill seeks to diminish what have been called by-law streets with little law and much monotony. It hopes to get rid of the regulation roads that are so regular that they lack that line of beauty which Hogarth said was in a curve. It seeks to improve the health of the people by raising the character of the house and the home and by extended inspection, supervision, direction and guidance of central control to help local authorities to do more than they do now'.[105] The Bill was finally passed as the Housing, Town

150 (*above*)
Norbury Estate. Paired entrances in Norton Gardens.
151 (*facing page*)
Norbury Estate. Paired entrances in Norton Gardens.

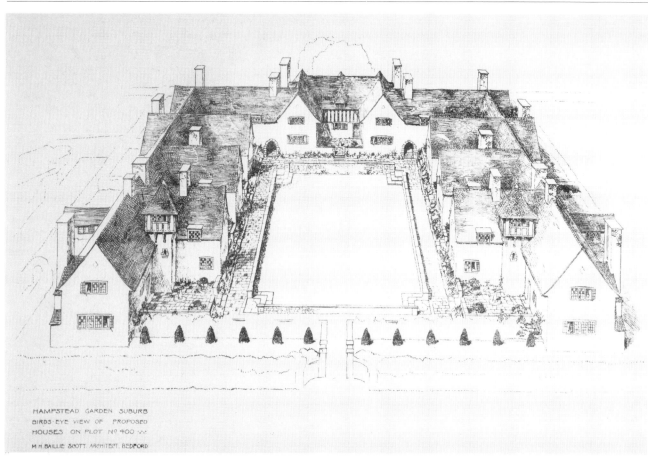

HAMPSTEAD GARDEN SUBURB
BIRDS-EYE VIEW OF PROPOSED
HOUSES ON PLOT Nº 400

M H BAILLIE SCOTT ARCHITECT, BEDFORD

152 *(top)*
Hampstead Garden Suburb. Proposed houses by M H Baillie Scott. From The British Architect, *20 November 1908.*
153 *(left)*
Norbury Estate. Quadrangle on Isham Road.
154 *(above)*
Norbury Estate. Quadrangle on Isham Road.

Planning, etc., Act 1909. In that same year Unwin published his *Town Planning in Practice* and Baillie Scott his *Town Planning and Modern Architecture at the Hampstead Garden Suburb*, while on the ground the main cottage area of the Suburb was already complete for all to see (Plate 156).

Another factor that helped to determine the character of the Old Oak Estate was the appointment of Archibald Stuart Soutar to its team of project architects. Born in 1879 in Arbroath, he was the brother of J C S Soutar who was to succeed Raymond Unwin in 1914 as supervising architect of Hampstead Garden Suburb, a position he held until his death thirty-four years later. In 1895 A S Soutar was articled to John Murray Robertson of Dundee and studied at Dundee University where he won the Queen's Prize in architecture. He started work in the Housing branch as a temporary assistant in 1901 but continued, throughout the decade, to collaborate with his brother: they made their names as town planning experts at this period in a series of successes in competitions for garden suburbs and model villages, including Woodlands, the Brodsworth Colliery Village near Doncaster, and the Ruislip Manor Estate of 1909. Archibald Soutar did not remain with the LCC long enough to achieve more than temporary status. None of the drawings for the Old Oak Estate dated 1912 and after is initialled by him: presumably he left before work began on the second contract for the western section. Both he and brother died in 1951.[106] Among the drawings initialled *A.S.S.* for the groups of cottages erected to the south of Erconwald Street are those for 268-274 Du Cane Road, dated April 1911 (Plate 157) and the adjacent 232-266, a terrace curved about a green planted with trees (Plate 158) and the two blocks that stand like handsome lodges at the junction of Du Cane Road and Fitzneal Street, architecturally the most important thoroughfare on the early part of the estate (Plates 159–

160). The assistants who worked closely with Soutar on the first contract were F J Lucas and J M Corment. Because Lucas, in common with most of his fellow architects at the Council, became a Licentiate of the RIBA in 1911 something is known of his background, but Corment remains undocumented in professional records except for the Council's note of his birth date, 1879, and the date of his engagement as a temporary assistant in the Architect's Department, July 1902.[107] It seems that he was never given permanent status but he continued to work on the western section until the outbreak of war. Among the drawings that carry his initials are those for the estate's shops. Frederick James Lucas, born in 1880, was articled from 1898 to 1901 to Colson, Farrow and Nisbett of London and Winchester, afterwards becoming an assistant in the firm. In 1902 he joined the office of J Morse-Smith in London and entered the Architect's Department later in the same year. On his RIBA Licentiate's declaration form Lucas stated that he had worked on block dwellings at the Bourne Estate and on cottages at White Hart Lane and Old Oak.[108] Drawings on which his initials appear include those for the rear elevations of 232-266 Du Cane Road but none relating to the second contract is marked by him and he must have left Council employment while still classed as temporary

155 *(top left)*
Old Oak Estate, Hammersmith. Plan showing complete estate with key to pre- and post-war development. From London Housing, *LCC, 1937, p 136.*
156 *(top right)*
Hampstead Garden Suburb. Plan of central cottage area. Reproduced from Town Planning in Practice, *in* The Legacy of Raymond Unwin, *ed Walter L Creese, 1967, fig 24.*

THE COTTAGE ESTATES 113

staff. Cottages for the area north of Erconwald Street seem to have been under the general control of John Sidney Brooks and J M Corment. Brooks, born in 1878, was articled to C G Baker in Bloomsbury from 1893 to 1895 and worked successively for Walter Millard, W H Harrison and, interestingly, J J Stevenson before entering the Housing branch in 1898. By the time he began work at Old Oak Brooks had been promoted to 1st class assistant and reached the top of his grade in January 1913. He was granted leave for military service and returned to the Council after the war to serve as a principal assistant architect until his retirement in 1940.[109]

Those cottages which can be directly linked with Archibald Soutar provide dramatic evidence of the homage that the whole western section of Old Oak pays to Hampstead Garden Suburb – homage not only to the Suburb as it was carried out but to the fantasy that lay behind it, the fairy-tale village tenderly portrayed in the illustrations to *Town Planning and Modern Architecture at the Hampstead Garden Suburb* (Plates 161–162). The deep quadrangles and closes, angle blocks and terraces unfolding along the line of a curving street or deliberately diverging from it show a scrupulous regard for the composite 'picture' to which they contribute, as if the Housing branch had set out to prove the strength of the book's central arguments. The planning of Fitzneal Street, for example (Plates 159, 163) may be seen as an impeccable response to Unwin's advice: 'Straight roads are apt to be unsuccessful

for want of any definition in the centre of the picture, hence it is desirable that the length of any such roads should not be too great without some break. The buildings may be brought forward at certain points to partially close and define the view and to replace by a portion of building standing approximately square with the line of vision a part of the street picture which would otherwise be filled with the fronts of the buildings seen in too acute perspective to be interesting'.[110]

The kind of decorative detail that enlivens and individualises the straight terraces of the earlier estates is much less evident at Old Oak. Doorways and gables, terraces and quadrangles are treated not as separate elements with their own identity but as interdependent parts of one complex and homogeneous architectural scheme. Paired entrances are tucked discreetly away behind plainly-moulded brick arches or obscured by trellises so as not to divert attention from the composition of their cottage-group (Plates 164–166). The estate lay-out itself had now become a more than sufficient source of picturesque interest and variety.

---

157 (*facing page, top*)
Old Oak Estate, 268–274 Du Cane Road.
158 (*facing page, bottom*)
Old Oak Estate, 232–266 Du Cane Road.
159 (*above*)
Old Oak Estate, Fitzneal Street from Du Cane Road. From an LCC photograph.

160 (*facing page, top*)
Old Oak Estate. Angle block, Fitzneal Street.
161 (*facing page, bottom*)
*Hampstead Garden Suburb. 'The Entrance to the Estate'.
From* Town Planning and Modern Architecture at the
Hampstead Garden Suburb, *Raymond Unwin and M H
Baillie Scott, 1909, p 12.*

162 (*top*)
*Hampstead Garden Suburb. 'A Corner House in Meadway'.
From* Town Planning and Modern Architecture at the
Hampstead Garden Suburb, *Raymond Unwin and M H
Baillie Scott, 1909, p 20.*
163 (*above*)
Old Oak Estate. Cottages in Fitzneal Street.

164 *(top)*
Old Oak Estate. Paired entrances, Du Cane Road.
165 *(left)*
Old Oak Estate. Paired entrances, Du Cane Road.
166 *(facing page)*
Old Oak Estate. Paired entrances, Du Cane Road.

Tile-hung gables here and there provide a rare variation of texture in the cottage elevations and dark red bricks and roof tiles give unity of colour. Unwin had stressed the importance of roofs in establishing the coherent, self-contained character of old English villages and had hoped to show, in his designs for Letchworth, that 'By keeping to roof tiles, a unity of effect is produced which in no other way could be so easily or completely attained. The securing of that degree of unity . . . allows greater freedom to be given in other respects, without injury to the whole effect'.[111] It is not surprising that Unwin's ideas were received with such sympathy in the Housing branch. They were the expression in planning terms of the very ideals upon which the branch's work had been based since the 1890s. The character of the Fitzneal Street quadrangle (Plate 167), with its tiled roofs and hipped dormers, owes as much to the architecture of Philip Webb and English vernacular tradition as to Unwin's theory and example. In their single-minded devotion to those ideals the architects of the LCC contrived to avoid the quaintness of expression and cloying sentimentality that constantly threatened the garden suburb ideal and did not leave even Hampstead unscathed.

Combining inventiveness with austerity in its design and breadth with intimacy in its planning, the Old Oak Estate is, perhaps, the LCC's finest contribution to the revival of English domestic architecture. Ironically, while the western section was in course of completion, that revival was already in rapid decline. Its epitaph was pronounced by Lethaby in 1915 when, in a curiously worded plea to English architects, he called upon them to look to Germany for new inspiration. England, he said, had arrived first at the idea of a free architecture 'which should develop in its own sphere, and not be forever casting back to disguise itself in the skins which it had long ago sloughed off – or, like the dog of Scripture, eat its dinner twice over'. German architects, exposed to the influence of the Arts and Crafts movement through Hermann Muthesius, had seized upon this idea, while in England it was now forgotten and architecture once again 'diverted and maimed and caged into formulas which (are) not only dead but never had life'.[112]

When the staff of the Architect's Department returned to the drawing board in 1919 the design themes of both cottages and flatted estates were taken up again where they had been abandoned. The elegance of the Roehampton Estate, begun in 1920, and certain early sections of post-war Old Oak is evidence, not of a renewal of inspiration, but of the richness of the stylistic resources that had been developed before 1914 and were now drawn upon for a time but no longer replenished. As far as flatted estates were concerned, no such reserves of energy remained. Among the last multi-storey blocks to be erected before the war were those at Tabard Street, Southwark, opened in 1916 (Plate 168). Already destitute of the individualist spirit of the earlier years, they predict the post-war development of LCC flat design as accurately as Linnell Close at Hampstead Garden Suburb foreshadows the formal terraces built at

Old Oak in 1919 (Plates 169–170). The capitulation of Council architects to an increasingly listless neo-Georgian revivalism was part of a national movement, the course of which neither Lethaby's warnings nor the hiatus of war had the power to halt. The character of LCC housing during the inter-war years was to be determined by a tacit agreement among architects grown weary or complacent that 'the gentler and finer instincts of men' could be more easily symbolised in the use of a bland and well-tried formula than in the harder search for original design.

167 (*facing page, top*)
Old Oak Estate. Quadrangle in Fitzneal Street.
168 (*facing page, bottom*)
Tabard Garden Estate, Southwark. Flats, 1916.
169 (*overleaf, top*)
Hampstead Garden Suburb. Linnell Close. From Town Planning and Modern Architecture at the Hampstead Garden Suburb, *Raymond Unwin and M H Baillie Scott, 1909, p 48.*
170 (*overleaf, bottom*)
Old Oak Estate, post-war development. 37-45 Wulfstan Street.

·NOTES·

1 GLRO, Metropolitan Board of Works, Minutes of Proceedings, 1861, p 148 (34).

2 Owen Fleming, 'The Rebuilding of the Boundary Street Estate', *RIBA Journal*, 7 April 1900, vol VII, p 272.

3 GLRO, *LCC Staff Gazette*, February 1905, p 19.

4 Joseph Chamberlain, 'Labourers' and Artisans' Dwellings', *Fortnightly Review*, December 1883, pp 767–8.

5 *Five Per Cent Philanthropy*, 1973, p 84.

6 *The Nether World*, 1889 (1973 reprint p 274).

7 Charles Booth, *Life and Labour of the People in London*, 1902 edition, first series: Poverty, vol 3, p 36.

8 *The Housing Problem in England*, 1907, p 231.

9 *The Housing Question in London*, LCC, 1900, p 170.

10 *Ibid*, p 47.

11 GLRO, Housing of the Working Classes Committee papers, report dated 18 November 1896.

12 GLRO, Public Health and Housing Committee minutes, 24 January 1893.

13 GLRO, Establishment Committee report, 7 March 1893.

14 W R Lethaby, Alfred H Powell and Frank L Griggs, *Ernest Gimson, his Life and Work*, 1924, p 4.

15 *The Builder*, 2 November 1895, vol 69, pp 312–3.

16 *AA Notes*, December 1895, vol X, p 113.

17 *The Housing Question in London*, LCC, 1900, p 192.

18 13 December 1890, vol 59, p 457.

19 11 October 1895, vol 44, p 252.

20 *Housing of the Working Classes in London*, LCC, 1913, p 36.

21 David Gregory Jones, 'Some Early Works of the LCC Architect's Department', *AA Journal*, November 1954, vol LXX, pp 96–7.

22 *The Builder*, 17 February 1900, vol 78, p 158.

23 RIBA Library, Recommendations . . . of Associates (9) 1891.

24 *AA Notes*, December 1888, vol III, p. 34.

25 *Magazine of Art*, 1893, vol XVI, p 94.

26 *LCC Staff Gazette*, June 1901, pp 71–2.

27 *The Builder*, 17 February 1900, vol 78, pp 158–9.

28 *RIBA Journal*, 7 April 1900, vol VII, p 273.

29 *The Builder*, 17 February 1900, vol 78, p 155.

30 GLRO, Housing of the Working Classes Committee papers, report by the Architect dated 1 November 1893.

31 *The Builder*, 17 February 1900, vol 78, p 159.

32 See, for example, *British Architect*, 26 February 1897, vol 47, p 146: '. . . suggestive in appearance of microbe propagation . . .'.

33 *RIBA Journal*, 7 April 1900, vol VII, p 265.

34 *Ibid*, p 268.

35 'Art as Applied to Town Schools', *Art Journal*, 1881, pp 137–140, 169–172.

36 *Ibid*, pp 170–1.

37 *British Architect*, 12 February 1897, vol 47, p 110.

38 All early LCC blocks of flats were originally known as 'Buildings', a term now generally abandoned for the less institutional title 'House'.

39 Vol 1, pp 203–4, plate 200.

40 RIBA Library, Recommendations . . . of Licentiates, 1911, no 1028.

41 GLRO, LCC Architect's Department, Register of Officers.

42 GLRO, *LCC Staff Gazette*, May 1908, p 68.

43 *RIBA Journal*, March 1945, vol. LII, pp 143–4.

44 Joyce Winmill, *Charles Canning Winmill*, 1946, p 22.

45 RIBA Library, Recommendations . . . of Licentiates, 1911, no 874.

46 *The Growth and Work of the RIBA 1834–1934*, ed J A Gotch, 1934, p 178.

47 *AA Notes*, April 1892, vol VI, pp 169–171.

48 *RIBA Journal*, March 1945, vol LII, pp 143–4.

49 *British Architect*, 26 February 1897, vol 47, p 146.

50 *British Architect*, 30 April 1897, vol 47, pp 306–7.

51 Joyce Winmill, *Charles Canning Winmill*, 1946, p 65.

52 March 1924, p 67.

53 12 March 1897, vol 47, p 180.

54 Biographical details principally from RIBA Library, Recommendations . . . of Licentiates, 1911, no 1011. See also *LCC Staff Gazette*, December 1915, p 200.

55 As expressed, for example, in *House Architecture*, 1880.

56 *On the Recent Reaction of Taste in English Architecture*, paper read before the General Conference of Architects, RIBA, 18 June, 1874, pp 6–8.

57 Letter from Winmill to Owen Fleming dated 29 July 1938, in the possession of Joyce Winmill.

58 *LCC Staff Gazette*, January 1916, pp 16–17.

59 RIBA Library, Recommendations . . . of Associates, 1892, no 117.

60 RIBA Library, biographical file, unidentified newspaper cutting.

61 RIBA Library, Recommendations . . . of Licentiates, 1911, no 919.

62 RIBA Library, biographical file.

63 *The Housing Question in London*, LCC, 1900, p 213.

64 *Ibid*, p 209.

65 *Ibid*, p 212.

66 *RIBA Journal*, 7 April 1900, vol VII, p 273.

67 R Williams, 'On Tenement-Houses for the Working Classes', *AA Notes*, January 1900, vol XV, pp 11–12.

68 14 May 1897, vol 47, p 343–4.

69 *RIBA Journal*, 7 April 1900, vol VII, p 250.

70 *The Housing Question in London*, LCC, 1900, pp 43–4.

71 *Life and Labour of the People in London*, 1902 edition, third series: Religious Influences, vol II, pp 68, 71.

72 Arthur Morrison, *A Child of the Jago*, 1896 (1969 reprint p 179).

73 *RIBA Journal*, 7 April 1900, vol VII, p 273.

74 Thomas Blashill's response to criticism of the Millbank competition by R Williams, an unsuccessful entrant, *AA Notes*, January 1900, vol XV, p 10.

75 *The Builder*, 17 February 1900, vol 78, p 160.

76 *AA Notes*, April 1900, vol XV, pp 54–5.

77 *Architectural Review*, 1905 (1), vol 17, p 248.

78 *The Builder*, 19 November 1937, vol 153, p 917.

79 *RIBA Journal*, 20 December 1937, vol XLV, p 204.

80 *RIBA Journal*, 24 January 1938, vol XLV, p 317.

81 RIBA Library, Recommendations . . . of Licentiates, 1911, no 882.

82 RIBA Library, Recommendations . . . of Licentiates, 1911, no 927; GLRO, LCC Architect's Department, Register of Officers.

83 David Gregory Jones, 'Some Early Works of the LCC Architect's Department', *AA Journal*, November 1954, vol LXX, p 101.

84 W R Lethaby, 'Some Northamptonshire Steeples', *Art Journal*, 1889, pp 255–6.

85 RIBA Library, Recommendations . . . of Associates, 1893, no 111; GLRO, LCC Architect's Department, Register of Officers; *Who's Who in Architecture*, 1914.

86 *Housing of the Working Classes in London*, LCC, 1913, p 88.

87 *RIBA Journal*, 24 April 1909, vol XVI, pp 415–7.

88 Biographical details principally from the obituary by Frederick Hiorns, *RIBA Journal*, June 1953, vol LX, p 347. See also GLRO, LCC Architect's Department, Register of Officers.

89 *British Architect*, 30 April 1909, vol 71, p 309.

90 GLRO, Housing of the Working Classes Committee Report, 23 November 1898.

91 From 'Art and Beauty of the Earth', 1881 (*The Collected Works of William Morris, vol XXII*, p 170).

92 *Housing of the Working Classes in London*, LCC, 1913, p 12.

93 *The Builder*, 9 November 1901, vol 81, pp 403–4.

94 This and subsequent quotations from the Tract, not always easily available in its original form, appear in the extracts reprinted in *The Legacy of Raymond Unwin*, ed Walter L Creese, 1967.

95 *Housing of the Working Classes in London*, LCC, 1913, p 72.

96 *The Letters of William Morris to his Family and Friends*, ed Philip Henderson, 1950, p 236.

97 *Book of Houses*, 1890, Introduction.

98 Biographical details principally from RIBA Library, biographical file and GLRO, LCC Architect's Department, Register of Officers.

99 *AA Notes*, May 1903, vol XVIII, p 67.

100 *RIBA Journal*, 24 April 1909, vol XVI, pp 441–2.

101 RIBA Library, Recommendations . . . of Associates, 1902, no 1438; *RIBA Journal*, April 1944, vol LI, p 158.

102 *British Architect*, 20 November 1908, vol 70, p 375.

103 RIBA Library, Recommendations . . . of Licentiates, 1911, no 1738; GLRO, LCC Architect's Department, Register of Officers.

104 RIBA Library, Recommendations . . . of Licentiates, 1910, no 229; GLRO, LCC Architect's Department, Register of Temporary Assistants.

105 *Housing of the Working Classes in London*, LCC, 1913, pp 14–15.

106 GLRO, LCC Architect's Department, Register of Temporary Assistants; RIBA Library, Recommendations . . . of Licentiates, 1911, no 924; biographical file.

107 GLRO, LCC Architect's Department, Register of Temporary Assistants.

108 *Ibid, loc cit.*; RIBA Library, Recommendations . . . of Licentiates, 1911, no 909.

109 RIBA Library, Recommendations . . . of Licentiates, 1911, no 961; GLRO, LCC Architect's Department, Register of Officers.

110 I have searched in vain among my notes for the source of this passage. However, its theme is recurrent in Unwin's writings. See, for example, *Town Planning in Practice*, 1909, pp 252–4.

111 Raymond Unwin, 'Cottage Building in Garden City', *The Garden City*, June 1906, vol 1, p 108.

112 'Modern German Architecture and what we may learn from it', *AA Journal*, February 1915, vol XXX, p 142.

·BIBLIOGRAPHY·

Charles Booth, *Life and Labour of the People in London*, 1902 edition.

Arthur Morrison, *A Child of the Jago*, 1896, reprinted 1969.

LCC, *The Housing Question in London:* Being an account of the Housing Work done by the Metropolitan Board of Works and the London County Council, between the years 1855 and 1900, with a summary of the Acts of Parliament under which they have worked. 1900.

Barry Parker and Raymond Unwin, *The Art of Building a Home*, 1901; *Cottage Plans and Common Sense* (Fabian Tract No 109), 1902.

Hermann Muthesius, *Das Englische Haus*, 1904.

Sydney Perks, *Residential Flats of all Classes*, 1905.

Ernest R Dewsnup, *The Housing Problem in England*, 1907.

Raymond Unwin, *Town Planning in Practice*, 1909.

Raymond Unwin and M H Baillie Scott, *Town Planning and Modern Architecture at the Hampstead Garden Suburb*, 1909.

LCC, *Housing of the Working Classes in London:* Notes on the action taken between the years 1855 and 1912 for the better housing of the working classes in London, with specific reference to the action taken by the London County Council between the years 1889 and 1912. 1913.

Ewart G Culpin, *The Garden City Movement Up-to-date*, 1913.

LCC, *London Housing*, 1937.

Joyce Winmill, *Charles Canning Winmill*, 1946.

Walter L Creese, *The Search for Environment;* The Garden City: Before and After, 1966.

ed Walter L Creese, *The Legacy of Raymond Unwin*, 1967.

J N Tarn, *Working Class Housing in 19th century Britain*, 1971; *Five per cent Philanthropy*, 1973.

A S Gray, Introduction to Letchworth Museum and Art Gallery exhibition catalogue, *Barry Parker, 1867–1947 and the First Garden City, 1903–1973*, 1973.

Susan Randall, *The LCC's Bellingham Estate* (unpublished thesis, University of Essex).

Edwardian Architecture and its origins, ed Alistair Service, 1975.

Articles

Thomas Blashill, 'Working Class Dwellings in Blocks', *The Builder*, 17 February 1900, vol 78, pp 155–158.

Owen Fleming, 'The Rebuilding of the Boundary Street Estate', *RIBA Journal*, 7 April 1900, vol VII, pp 264–273.

W E Riley, 'The Architectural Work of the LCC', *RIBA Journal*, 24 April 1909, vol XVI, pp 413–438.

David Gregory Jones, 'Some Early Works of the LCC Architect's Department', *AA Journal*, November 1954, vol 70, pp 95–105.

R Vladimir Steffel, 'The Boundary Street Estate', *Town Planning Review*, April 1976, vol 47, No 2, pp 161–173.

·INDEX·

126